HUMANITY UNVEILED

DR. ARIEL R. KING

A COLLECTION OF
UNEXPECTED ENCOUNTERS
THAT REVEAL THE HUMAN
SPIRIT IN US ALL

Copyright @ 2024 by Dr. Ariel Rosita King, Dr King Solutions Inc.
All rights reserved.

Published by the Ariana-Leilani Children's Foundation
and Dr King Solutions, Washington, DC

Published simultaneously in Canada

Published simultaneously in United Kingdom

All rights reserved. No part of this publication may be reproduced, used, performed, stored in a retrieval system, or transmitted in any form or by any means, electronic, mechanical, photocopying, recording or otherwise except as permitted by Section 107 and 108 of the 1976 United States Copyright Act without the prior written permission of the author Dr. Ariel Rosita King, the Publisher, if living, except for critical articles or reviews and certain other noncommercial uses permitted by copyright law. Copyright authorization through payment of the appropriate pre-copy fee to the Copyright Clearance Center Inc
(www.copyright.com).

Requests to the publisher for permission should be addressed online at http://www.drkingsolutions.com/book/permission .

Library of Congress Cataloging-in-Publication Data is available.

ISBN: 9781958662069 (Hardcover)

ISBN: 9781958662076 (Softcover)

ISBN: 978-1-958662-13-7 (Audiobook)

Cover Design: Tri Widyatmaka

Interior Design: Ogunbiyi Ismail

Author Photo ©: Julio Igelsias

Dedication

Dedicate to all the people worldwide who are the breath of our collective humanity and to the Legacy of Family.

Dr Ariel Rosita King's Grandmother, Gloria Swanson Jefferson King; Mother, Dr. Margo G. King, Daughters, Ariana-Leilani Margarita Alexandra King-Pfeiffer, and Vicky Anya King.

Contents

Dedication 5

Preface 9

Introduction 15

SECTION I: IF I AM NOT FOR MYSELF, WHO WILL BE FOR ME?
Inward View of Humanity

1. Humanity is Confidence 23
   Dr. Nina Simone – USA / France

2. Humanity is Authenticity 29
   Lauderic Rex Caton - Trinidad & Tabago

3. Humanity is Resilience 39
   His Excellency Thong Khon - Cambodia

4. Humanity is Value 45
   Alice Lucille Coltrane – USA (aka Swamini Turiyasangitananda)

SECTION II: IF I AM ONLY FOR MYSELF, WHAT AM I
Humanity Connection - Civility, Respect, Championing

5. Humanity is Civility 53
   HRH The Princess Royal, United Kingdom

6. Humanity is Respect 63
   Dr. Maya Angelou

7. Humanity is Championing 73
   H. E. Ambassador Alfonso E. Lenhardt, USA

8. Humanity is Opportunity 81
   H.E. Ambassador Henry David Owen - USA

9. Humanity is Forgiveness 87
   Archbishop Desmond Tutu – South Africa

10. Humanity is Compassion 93
    Pope Francis – Vatican

SECTION III: IF NOT NOW, THEN WHEN?
Humanity Now

11. Humanity is Joy 101
    Dr. Cornel West – USA

12. Humanity is Connection 109
    Cyril Thomson Mitchell - Scotland

13. Humanity is Kindness 117
    Corrine Dettmeijer- Vermuelen, Netherlands

14. Humanity is Humility 123
    President Frederik Willem De Klerk, South Africa

SECTION IV: IF NOT ME, THEN WHO?
(Dr Ariel KING)

15. Humanity is Compassion 131
    Dr. Elizabeth Kubler-Ross Switzerland/ USA

16. Humanity is Courage 139
    Dr. Matthew Raphael McVarish - Scotland

17. Humanity is Consideration 147
    President Nelson Mandela, South Africa

18. Humanity is Legacy 155
    Dr. Margo G. King

19. Humanity is Life 163
    Conclusion

About The Author 169

Preface

WHO WOULD HAVE THE HUTZPAH, the audacity to look at such a broad, and ethereal topic as "H-U-M-A-N-I-T-Y?"

Can I share with you that you aren't the only one who had this thought? There is a thought that something as broad, as vast as humanity, is not a subject matter that a singular book could contain, or a singular person could attempt to put into a context to understand how it fits into our daily lives, not for some but for everyone.

Humanity is such a big subject that is difficult to simply define, but we know when we see it, and especially when we experience it. The topic of humanity is easy to say that it is a topic that one should avoid, unless one is a philosopher, clergy, or someone who believes that naming and recognizing our shared humanity is the foundation of life. We are brave, and audacious to believe that one small act can bring more humanity into this world.

It is for this reason why the book you are holding isn't just a thought in my imagination but something I had to brainstorm.

The need put the "who am I" to talk about humanity to the side, because I firmly believe is a "who am I" in us all, and that "I" is desperate to be seen, felt, heard, expressed, and championed, more importantly desires to connect so that "I" and "We" can exist all in one. For humanity exists and is expressed in both the I and We.

I will not be long-winded in my explanation of this book, but I will do it because I believe it is important for us to understand that the human connection is not an "it would be nice" idea or construct, but it is the essence of who we are, who we were, and who we would like to see in our tomorrows. From wars to poverty to rising suicide rates, we have seen the collection of ignoring this problem of us living fully as humans in our collective humanity. Add to the mix the addition of artificial intelligence and the constant rise of social media; it is easy to see how if we do not stand in the gap, it will only widen, and the hope for a world filled with compassion for ourselves and others will cease to exist, and that is something we can ill afford.

Now you are probably wondering why I care about this topic so much, especially being that I've lived quite a few years, seen almost more countries than most people could even fathom, and probably in my young age, it would be a lot easier to tackle a subject that is easy to fathom or easily explore.

Well, if I had it my way, I would not have written this book. There are many book ideas I have that one would call low-hanging fruit that I could have tackled, but this book found my curiosity and would demand exploration. It became quite clear that as I look back on my life, this call for writing this book has always been a part of my life. The ringing to explore this topic has never stopped. I cannot explain why I've been called, but finding a solution to why isn't something that will close the gap in our world being more human.

So what will? Perhaps hearing stories of how humanity was unveiled to me through interesting and unexpected encounters with people who did not have to show me the grace, the love, the care that they did when they met me. From people like Dr. Maya Angelou, whom I met after an event and spoke to personally, to my random encounter at baggage claim with Dr. Nina Simone, or the meeting with President Nelson Mandela that didn't happen, but the note he wrote to me did and how it showed me that I wasn't just an encounter or an appointment on a calendar but more so I was a person who had value and deserved courtesy like every other important person.

These people showed me that we are all VIPs (Very Important People), and us losing that sense of wonder, civility, respect for one another has us treating animals more humane than we do humans; truly sad and shocking.

So today I come to you to share over 18 encounters I've had with people who have pulled back the curtain and all showed me an element of humanity that I believe will help you and me both to apply the lessons that resonate with us from these encounters to make the world more compassionate, more loving, and have the connection we've always were meant to have and the understanding of our common humanity.

Before we move into the actual book and principles in it that can help us connect more, it's important I share with you who this book is for and who this book isn't for because I believe that time is a limited resource and I would hate for you to waste yours on a book that you may never use or may not be ready to use.

Let me begin by sharing who this book isn't for. If you are someone who feels as though you may know all there is to know about being kind, being more human, and feel like your mindset is fixed and not open to seeing alternative perspectives that can enrich your understanding, you have my full permission to exit left and pass this book to someone else. Now I will warn you that it might be something you regret later on, but that is fully your right and one that I respect.

My hope is you are a part of the group that is curious to know what has this person who has met some interesting figures learned about humanity from them and more so, is there a chance that I can be 1% better as a human and transfer that 1%

to others and create a chain reaction that creates ripples of love and kindness, compassion and respect in my small world and see it expand to even greater heights and spaces?

If that is you, can I just give you the warmest embrace even right now? I wrote this book for leaders and seekers who are look consistently to contribute in the world in order to leave it better than the way they found it. One small act of kindness, humanity, will cause a ripple in the ethical arch that surrounds us. When humanity is seen or felt it causes an energy that perpetuates itself. Humanity perpetuates itself to another act that ultimately forms a link of humanity that is so strong that it reverberates positive energy wherever it is uncovered.

Being human is about learning and knowing about ourselves, loving ourselves, and the passing it on to others in any way every day. Do you realize how many people are depressed right now and don't know which way is forward? And they're doing everything they can to try to figure out how to make life better. "Maybe if I have these clothes, or maybe if I get this particular friend, or maybe if I get this particular car, or maybe if I try this particular wine, or maybe if I get this particular boyfriend, or girlfriend, or this kind of wife or this kind of husband." And we're all looking, we're searching. And what's amazing is that everything we're searching for is already within us. Waiting for Godot. Right? We are Godot, we are waiting for ourselves to see and recognise what is already inside of us.

If we spend half the time searching within ourselves and figuring out who we are, then we do not need to look for our humanity outside, we'd be incredible people. But you know what? We'd be dangerous, too. Many people want us to look outside, of ourselves because that's a wonderful way to manipulate and control who we are and what we do. By always looking outside for everything, we forget that everything we need is already in us. We are born with humanity.

That is the opportunity that this book invites you on, and I hope by the end of it that 1% will change you as it has changed me forever and that you will join me in championing others to fully know thyself and be true and invite others to do the same.

Thank you in advance for joining me on this tall task, revealing humanity. It can't be climbed without each of us giving one another a boost. This book is that first boost, and I hope that by the end of this book, you will take it further than I could have ever imagined.

To this hope being realised, let us begin.

Introduction

Where does one begin to tackle such a topic as humanity? I mention tackling because it appears that humanity has been quite elusive since almost the beginning of time. We all have some idea of what humanity is, but the question I'm left pondering and looking to help both you and I grasp is what humanity is, where is humanity, and how do we unveil humanity, and share it with the world.

When the conversation of humanity is brought up, we often have images of things like the United Nations, World Peace, War, people being together, exploration, and the study of human beings, just to name a few. While none of these are not part of the conversation, I firmly believe that humanity cannot be seen, captured, or shared if one important starting point is established. That point is the establishment of humanity within oneself.

Humanity before it can be given to someone, needs to be in the possession of someone first. This is a part of the conversation that is not covered enough and it's the reason why I firmly believe that the approach to us being more human has been like putting a circle peg in a square hole. We think of great figures like Mother Theresa and how giving she was of herself, how much of a humanitarian she was, but what we do not talk about enough is what was her relationship with herself that would allow her to have the capacity to see the humanity in ours and not get burnt out or feel defeated despite not seeing others do the same around her?

If humanity is to be unveiled, the first layer of that process is being able to see yourself and having others see you too. Taking it a step further, I like to call it "championing me". How does one champion themselves? What does that look like and how does that help us to unveil humanity? Let's dive in and talk about it.

Before we can talk about championing ourselves, we must understand the landscape of this thought and what gets in the way of this happening already. When taking inventory, championing yourself is not a common thing, unfortunately. According to the World Health Organization (WHO), suicide was the 17th leading cause of death globally in 2019. According to the National Institute of Mental Health (NIMH) in the United States, suicide was the 10th leading cause of death.

Shockingly, suicide is also one of the was top 3 in leading causes of death for young people between 15-24 years old!

These stats are staggering. What would lead a human being to stop wanting to be? Why instead of championing, they went in the complete opposite direction? Before we can solve problems like world hunger, world peace, and all the other cute stuff that we hear people say when they are in front of a group of people and want to be seen as just and righteous, we must understand why someone is not championing themselves. Until we do so, the gap that exists in our abilities to champion others will remain wider than that Grand Canyon.

Humanity, Hidden in Plain Sight

Humanity is hidden in plain sight. But it's almost like saying, well, I don't find the humanity. I don't know what you're talking about, you tell me that I can see and experience humanity, but I don't. Interestingly, when in pursuing it directly, it's difficult to experience or see. But if you put yourself in the position of a giver or being a person that is involved rather than a bystander, then humanity it's much easier to be a part of your life. I believe that these encounters of experiencing humanity are not just the same for everyone. The experiences and the way we experience humanity is unique to us. Humanity experienced by us is just for us. The encounter of humanity uniquely speaks to you and is there uniquely for you. Since you are unique, your experiences in humanity can never duplicated.

Everybody has different experiences and humanity language. For somebody to meet or have experiences with the same person, could not have the same humanitarian affect. Each experience in humanity is unique to the people, place, time, personality, experiences, and expectations.

The encounters you have with humanity and the ones that I have with the stories generated from the encounters with grace happens interactions will never be the same or be experienced in the same way for two people. Humanity in interactions with us, others and is a specific place and time is unique. For this uniqueness is the exact reason that our experience and engagement of humanity is such a personalised gift.

Humanity starts with getting to know who you are, and what's important to you. Humanity does not start with other people, and what they think, or say about you on social media, your family and social circles. Who are you when the lights are out and there's nobody there to confirm who you are? What's the most important to you? If you're stripped of everything, what do you have to say is this is my bare minimum, this is what I must be left in my life. I am not talking about things. I'm talking about who you are, and what's important to you, and how your life is supposed to go.

I think that the reason that I have met various historical people the way I have, without direct intention is because I've been able to give myself grace and an attitude that I do not want or need to try to reach perfection. "I'm a full human being". I basically like who I am I don't care if you like me no., I hope you do. But if you're not, I'm okay with that, and this self-comfort, (If I am not for myself, who will be for me?) leads to confidence. The confidence does not come from a place of feeling as if I'm the best, or I'm the greatest. That confidence come from, I know who I am and I'm good with it, I accept full imperfect self.

People call it being comfortable in your own skin, which is a strange thing to say, why wouldn't you be comfortable in your skin? It is your skin. Whose skin would you be comfortable in?

Many of us are taught by people in our lives to look outside of ourselves for that validation. When we are sure of who we are and we are for ourselves, this outside validation can be positive and inspiring.

Yet, if we do not truly know who we are, and are not for ourselves, when we seek validation, it is usually from our social circles, including online circles. All we are all looking for is affirmation of our humanity, of being fully human in different places and ways. Someone to say in some way, "I see you; I acknowledge you, I'm glad you're here on earth, and the world really needs you, you are important, your existence is important, and the world could not do without you. It's that simple.

Many of us are stressed daily trying to figure out with everyone, and everything that we're doing, how we can get back to that bliss, the humanity of who we are, not understanding that it's already there, it just must be uncovered. Humanity, right here with you, now, hidden in plain sight. Humanity is not a one size fit all. There is no right or wrong way to allow yourself the grace of being a part of humanity. Humanity is your birth right. It is always with you, for you, and allows for active participation to be appreciated and multiplied.

The book has four main sections with stories of encounters that remind, teach, solidify and celebrates our collective humanity.

The principal of an ancient philosopher Hillel a simple way to see humanity

If I am not for myself, who will be for me?

If I am only for myself, what am I?

If not now, then when? – Hillel

If not me, then who? - King

I decided that through my life experiences that taking personal responsibility for action is needed. Thus, I added a fourth part.

SECTION I

IF I AM NOT FOR MYSELF, WHO WILL BE FOR ME?

Inward View of Humanity

Chapter One - Confidence
Dr Nina Simone - France, USA

Chapter Two - Authenticity
Lauderic Rex Caton - Trinidad and Tobago, UK

Chapter Three - Resilience
Minister Thong Khon - Cambodia

Chapter Four – Value
Alice Lucille Coltrane
(aka Swamini Turiyasangitananda) USA

.

1

Humanity is Confidence.

Dr. Nina Simone – USA / France

IN THE GENTLE CADENCE OF OUR DIALOGUE, THE TALE OF MY ENCOUNTER with Dr. Nina Simone unfurled like a delicate tapestry woven from chance and curiosity.

"I believe our encounter was fated to be brief," I began, reminiscing about the bustling baggage claim as we arrived from Geneva to Los Angeles Airport (LAX) where our paths intersected. The mundane setting belied the significance of the moment, as I found myself engaged in conversation with a stranger, oblivious to her being renowned.

Dr Nina Simone had travelled from her home in Europe with her large dog. As I waited for my baggage a crate was bought the baggage claim area with a large black and white dog. I was curious to see if the dog was okay since it was an extremely long flight. Without much introspection I bent down started speaking to the dog, and reassuring it, petting it, and we forgot about everyone else. The spark ignited when I spoke with her dog, I recalled, a smile playing at the corners of my lips. It was as if fate orchestrated our meeting through a chance interaction.

Dr. Simone's commanding presence demanded authenticity—a demand I met with unwavering honesty, even amidst vulnerability. As I rose up I saw a woman in a wheel chair. "She invited the encounter, even in a state of disarray," I mused, reflecting on the paradox of courage intertwined with vulnerability. She said, with great command and deep commanding voice: "And WHO are you?!!!" Understanding that I must answer with care and humility, I said "Hi, my name is Ariel Rosita King. May I ask your name?" She said, "My name is Dr Nina Simone"!

Dr. Simone's presence exuded a strong sense of self and resilience, despite the physical and emotional exhaustion and vulnerability as she sat waiting in a wheelchair. Amidst the chaos of the long flight and travel, she shared fragments of her life; tales of a cherished home for over 20 years on the French border near Switzerland, tinged with the bittersweet of temporarily leaving her home in France.

The unknown anticipation of returning temporarily for reigniting her career to her roots in America. Dr Nina Simone said that going back to the USA, was not planned, but necessary after having a heated disagreement with her neighbor in France. She was not sure if the USA she had left behind in 1973, was the same in the 1990s.

As she spoke, I glimpsed the contours of courage etched into her choices including her expat life in France. We spoke about her love for swimming every day and her garden. We talked about the differences of living in the USA and France as a woman of African descent. A courage that embraced vulnerability without flinching, a courage that dared to confront fears head-on, while integrating the challenged into the tapestry of her life.

In her story, I found echoes of my own journey; a journey propelled by the belief that embracing discomfort is the crucible of growth. I understood Dr Nina Simone, in her life choices pursued as an expat in France while travelling the world. Her need to be understood, valued, and authentic gave me a glimpse into the life I could choose too. Dr Simone had confidence in herself, her choices, and her life, without being pre-occupied with the way she looked. Or even what others thought. She was fully and unapologetically herself!

Dr Nina Simone in her last days in her home in Carry-le-Rouet, France
(Image: Getty)

I had somehow found a kindred spirit, in the most unlikely of places. I believe chaos and crisis equals opportunity," I confessed, the words resonating with newfound clarity. "To navigate uncertainty is to chart a course towards self-discovery and transformation. As on the other side of fear and stagnation is opportunity." I was given a business card and she told me to call her when she settled into her new home and life in the US.

As our unexpected casual conversation ended, leaving behind a trail of lessons learned and stories untold, yet a knowing we both shared is a testament to the power of human connection that can and does happen anywhere at any time. When the connection happens, it allows for a transformative journey we embark upon, one encounter at a time.

Together, we delved deeper into the tapestry of encounters, extracting lessons and insights that transcended the boundaries of time and space. Dr Nina Simone, regardless of the chaos of change showed her Humanity in full view of her confidence to be herself.

2

Humanity is Authenticity

Lauderic Rex Caton - Trinidad & Tabago

As I sit here reflecting on the extraordinary life of my adopted Uncle Lauderic Rex Caton, memories flood my mind like an unstoppable tide. Lauderic Rex Caton, or Uncle Lauderic as I called him, was not just a figure from history as being the first to apply electricity to amplify the guitar, a jazz legend, and an intellectual renaissance man. He was, and continues to be a profound presence in my life, a beacon of wisdom, kindness, and curiosity in a world often clouded by confusion and exploitation.

You see, the stories you may have heard about Lauderic Rex Caton are only fragments of both truth and fiction, distorted by those who knew of him, but truly never knew him. People like Val Vilma, who claimed to be his friend, and understand him, but only sought to use his legacy for personal gain. She wrote that he as a hermit, a recluse who shunned human contact, and a hoarder. Yet, the reality was opposite, and nothing could be further from the truth. Most people do not know he was married his entire life and waited at their apartment until his death for his wife to return one day.

I remember the first time our paths crossed, during my time as a PhD student at the London School of Hygiene and Tropical Medicine, The University of London student apartment in Russel Square, Bloomsbury area of London. It was a serendipitous encounter, sparked by a simple act of kindness: gifting mugs to my 3 elderly next-door neighbors (4 Handel Street, NW, London), including Lauderic Rex Caton. I added my business card with my contact information in the mugs. Lauderic Caton contacted me and said that he was fascinated by this girl who already has 3 university degrees and wanted to know more about me. We set up a meeting to talk, and from that moment on, our lives intertwined in a beautiful dance of discovery, friendship, adopted family and mutual love and respect.

Uncle Lauderic was a man fascinated by electrical engineering, maths, languages (he even wrote in Sanskrit), and technology, by the intricacies of life, and by the beauty of music.

He didn't talk much about his achievements or his past with exception of his dear sister in Trinidad and Tobago. Instead, he shared moments of joy and laughter, as he had a wicked sense of humour. We also had spirited debates about anything and everything. He especially enjoyed being in the company with other international young people from University of London. He even made friends with my friend, Dr. George Haulthausen, who become his GP Physician, and an advocate for him too.

Lauderic Rex Caton Kissing Baby Nandi, my cousin in London

Uncle Lauderic, and me shared a love of learning, curiosity and family, times of quiet contemplation, and open invitations shared pot-luck meals and Bar-B-Q's with others at my garden apartment. Day to day, Uncle Lauderic said I became the "daughter I never had" and I felt that he was one of the most important males in my life. I was committed to Uncle Lauderic and with time helped with all in his daily life, while also helping him to research, preserve his professional and historical legacy, while protecting him from predators.

Uncle Lauderic was a vegetarian, a yogi, a extremely fit and mentally sharp 88-year-old. He had stomach pains and stopped eating the food I had delivered daily. I asked our mutual GP friend to look after him while I was doing my PhD field research in South Africa. When I returned, I took him to be evaluated. He had a mass in his stomach. He was admitted to the hospital and test revealed that he had cancer of the stomach. I, as his legal representative and only active family member returned to the hospital each day for several weeks.

My Uncle Lauderic was a true intellectual! He was going to have surgery and I was assured that they would keep me informed. I flew back to South Africa, and as soon as I arrived at my second home and called him. He said that he was being released from the hospital. I was shocked, called the hospital, and asked them to wait for me to fly back to London that evening. I arrived in London that morning after a 13-hour flight and went straight to the hospital to see Uncle Lauderic. He was sitting up in bed writing in Sanskrit and doing complicated math. I was relieved!

Dr Ariel King, Lauderic Rex Caton and friends from University of London

The doctor pulled me aside and said he had up to 6 months to live. I quickly called his family in Trinidad, the UK home office to get a passport for him so that we could fulfill his wishes to go see his older sister, Ortelia and for us to spend his last days with his family in Trinidad. I quickly learned that after more than 50 years in Britain, Uncle Lauderic did not change to UK citizenship. That day, the hospital doctor and nurses gave permission for Uncle Lauderic and me to go to get passport photos taken.

He put on his clothes, and a Barret, we left the hospital and slowly walked to the photo shop. Photos were taken, with and without his black Barret, with a huge radiant smile. At the hospital that afternoon, as he slept from exhaustion from our walk, I left him to take care of all tasks needed to bring him back home to Trinidad and Tabego. That early morning as I tried to sleep in his bed I tossed and turned uneasy. Finally, I called the nurses station and asked how Uncle Lauderic was doing.

Lauderic Rex Caton Passport photo with Barret taken the day before his death.

I was told that they were trying to call me because Uncle Lauderic was asking for me to come and was in a lot of pain. I dressed quickly and ran all the way to the hospital, in 15 minutes. When I arrived on the unit Uncle Lauderic turned looked at me and stop groaning to say, "Hi Sweetie-pie!" Then he groaned in severe pain. Within less than 10 minutes of my arrival, his stomach ruptured, and he passed away while I held his hand, stroked his face, and told him how much I loved him, and I would always be there for him. I was so thankful that he waited for me to come and be with him as he passed away. What an amazing gift!

As an adopted family member with legal responsibility, my name was added to his death certificate as witness to his transition. Now, I had to do all I could to preserve his history, memory, and items. Uncle Lauderic feared very little and few people. Yet he was extremely afraid that Val Wilmar, after not returning his passport, would go into his apartment and take all the items for a museum collection she was making from the belongings of Jazz Musicians. Thus, one of my first tasks with the help of others who loved Uncle Lauderic was to go through his apartment and gather all the items of historical significance to be preserved for history and future generations.

I was able to find a beautiful coffin with music notes and instruments carved into it. I made a reservation to fly back from London to Trinidad with Uncle Lauderic's body. I arrived and his family welcomed me as family. With assistance I organised the funeral, the burial plot and stone, the death and funeral announcement, the food afterwards, and to give the family the left-over funds that he left for them. I decided that I did not need monetary resources from my Uncle Lauderic because he have me the best gift of all – his time, trust, and love.

Lauderic Rex Caton at funeral in Trinidad and Tobago with family and me his "adopted daughter," Dr Ariel King on 13 February 1999.

Beyond his musical and intellectual genius, and his many accomplishments, Uncle Lauderic taught me a profound lesson about hope, unconditional love, and renewal. No matter how dark the night may seem, there is always a glimmer of light on the horizon. He showed me that relationships can be renewed, that life can be lived with wonder, purpose, and joy, even in the face of adversity.

So, as I continue to preserve his legacy, cherishing his love letters to his wife, while he was a traveling musician, his novels:

The Transposition, and Viola, and a handwritten original symphony, called "The Sepia" that was accepted by the BBC to be played live on the radio, until they found that he was a "jazz musician."

I do so with a sense of gratitude for having loved him and known him. Mr. Lauderic Rex Caton was more than just a jazz pioneer; a symphony composer, an author, an intellectual and yogi, he was family, a friend, and a mentor. The love and lessons from our relationship continues to be a guiding light in my life for which I will be eternally grateful.

3

Humanity is Resilience

His Excellency Thong Khon - Cambodia

As I reflect on my life changing time with H.E. Minister Thong Khon and his family from Cambodia, I'm reminded of the integration of connections from various aspects of my life as the founder and President of Ariel Foundation International since 2000.

I first met Minister Thong through one of our young ARIEL FOUNDATION INTERNATIONAL Changemakers, Sir Jayson

Thun Thong tai Thong was a participant of Ariel Foundation International Side Event at the Human Rights Council at the United Nations in Geneva. After the event, and its publication, Sir Jayson Thun Thong remained a young person who was part of the youth led events for Ariel Foundation International.

After several Ariel Foundation International events in Geneva and London we talked about having an event for youth in Cambodia. Little did I know at the time, that Sir Jayson Thun Thong and his family had a profound impact on my life waiting for me in Cambodia.

Sir Jayson Thun Thong ,as his given name, and me had a vision for bringing Ariel Foundation International to Cambodia, and several years later, after participating in several talks, presentations, and UN Summits, after many years our dream became a reality.

Through Ariel Foundation International, its/ former Chair, Ambassador Joseph Huggins, my youngest daughter Vicky, and me travelled to Cambodia with a personal invitation and an amazing travel and planned programme that allowed us to personally meet people from charities, businesses, government, and children.

What unfolded during our visit was beyond what I could have anticipated. H.E. Minister Thong, whose official role as Minister of Tourism, welcomed us to Cambodia with open arms alongside his wife, and family.

We arrived at a hotel and were led to a private dining room. I expected that Minister Thong was going to be formal and follow the formal protocol, as I am used to it in my meetings with various high level government officials. Instead, when I went into the private dining room, he hugged and kissed me. I was happily a little stunned because my thinking was diplomatic formal. Also, Sir Jayson Thun Thong's mother did the same, she gave me a warm hug and kiss. I felt as if I was welcomed by family. We sat down at a beautiful formal setting. They asked me if I could speak French. I said yes. Minister Thong started to speak French to me.

Minister Thong was a medical student in France his last year when he had to return to Cambodia. He and I started to speak in French together, rather than English. Minister Thong had to abandon his dream of being a physician, due to political upheaval in Cambodia. Yet, his commitment to assisting with health of the people, and improving healthcare endured. He utilises his position to advocate for better tourism that helps with funds and possibilities for investment in Cambodia's healthcare and access for its' people.

Mrs. Men Bunthoeun Thong also had a powerful story in the Cambodian war. She recounted her harrowing experiences in a prison camp with her infant daughter during the Khmer Rouge regime. She was relentless in to safeguarding her infant daughter, who is now a mother herself, from ultimate harm. Her resilience and resourcefulness were evident as she navigated the darkest of circumstances to ensure her family's survival.

On a humanity tour we were walking with Sir Jayson Thun Thong, and his mother in this place that was called the killing fields in Phnom Penh. As I walked on the path on the side, I then see the dirt has cloth and some bones. It is still there today as you're walking on top of these things. She's told me that "this is the camp I was in. As we walked, she told me how she was able to use her business skills to not just survive and to feed herself and to feed her daughter, but to make sure that her daughter was safe from elimination. Once this time in history was over, Mrs. Men Bunthoeun's daughter survived, was educated, and became a woman who had a child of her own. Then her dream was to have her son, Sir Jayson Thun Thong . This young man who gets to live in freedom, a young man who is the pride of the new Cambodia.

Now the Thong family who had not just dreams delayed but had to go through Cambodia at a time when they had to survive, the Khmer Rouge. This new son was their hope and dreams for New Cambodia, a new life, a new start to their shared humanity. They're getting back to being human again and knowing that they're human when they were treated less than human.

Walking through Cambodia, I witnessed firsthand the nation's commitment to preserving its painful history, that is enshrined in every step taken, a stark contrast to history of other countries that seek to bury and forget their past. Despite the atrocities they endured, the Cambodian people embraced forgiveness, a testament to their unwavering humanity.

The encounter left me deeply moved, grappling with the complexities of forgiveness and restoration. Mrs. Thong's analogy of broken China resonated profoundly, emphasizing the transformative power of restoration.

As I contemplate the impact of our meeting, I'm struck by the potential for leveraging everyday objects as vessels of healing and restoration. Perhaps there lies an opportunity to launch a brand centered around the concept of "Restore," where brokenness is celebrated as a testament to resilience and renewal.

In Minister Thong and his family, I found not only a remarkable story of survival but also a profound lesson in the enduring power of forgiveness and restoration. Their story serves as a poignant reminder that amidst the darkest of times, humanity's capacity for compassion and healing endures.

Mrs. Bunthoeun Men Thong, Dr Ariel King, and H.E. Minister Thong Khon

H.E. Minister Thong gives Dr Ariel King an official gift from Ministry of Tourism, Mrs. Mrs. Bunthoeun Men Thong, and Jayson Thun Thong in Cambodia at welcome lunch.

4

Humanity is Value

Alice Lucille Coltrane – USA (aka Swamini Turiyasangitananda)

Mrs. Alice Lucille Coltrane, a jazz pianist and harpist, later in life known as Swamini Turiyasangitananda had was a very brief, yet important part of my life through memories that have lasted for more than half century. Most people in the world know her as a musician in her own right, and the wife of the famous Jazz Saxophone player, John Coltrane, who had passed away in 1966. I didn't understand death, I only understood her husband was no longer there, and she worked making clothes.

My mother was in her early 20s and in the local Queens College. She needed another family in walking distance of our home and school to help care for me after school. We found an amazing family, The Jacksons John, Lavern, her mother and their two daughters my age Charlene and Danielle. I spent most my days after school and holidays at the Jackson's family. The three-story middle-class house with a front garden with trees and a back garden was always filled with people and activities. The basement had a full home business of a full clothing design business called Kawat Asilia that made Dakshikis (West African inspired V neck shirts and dresses).

Mrs. Coltrane, as I knew her, was one of the designers at this company. Despite her own challenges—being a widow with three boys, she was always kind to me. I remember her involving me in the process of making the Dashikis. She would patiently show me how to mark the material and choose fabrics. It was a different time, most done by hand, except when of using a sewing machine to sew the larger pieces together.

As a girl 5 or 6 years old as a person who thought I was capable and talented like her 1968-1969. I knew Mrs. Coltrane was a designer and seamstress and the only person who engaged and involved me in making clothes. She, like me, was there every day. Sometimes the Coltrane's two older sons, John Jr and Ravi who were my age would come and were my reluctant playmates for my favorite game, "house"! Oranyan, her younger son, was just a toddler, so we had no interest in playing with him.

The Jackson Family, Lavern with daughters Charlene & Daniel, son, and Mother. Teenager Ariel Rosita King on step of house in Quests, New York, where Kohat Alisia Fashion made.

Mrs. Coltrane was always so kind to me, and patient with me. Her smile brought me warmth, acceptance, and kindness as a mother. I would go downstairs to the Dakshiki production area and ask a lot of questions and just watch. Her patience and centeredness were exceptional. So much so that even as I child I recognised it. Sometimes I couldn't understand it because most people found me to be too active and asked too many questions.

Mrs. Coltrane would get the African fabrics, materials, cut the patterns, sew them together and add all the exceptional designs that make them Dashiki's unique. Yet, she would ask, "do you want to come in watch this, let me show you what I'm doing." Mrs. Coltrane would show me how to use the square yellow and white markers that we used to trace the patterns on the clothe to be cut. But this is how you can mark material without seeing when you need to cut it. So, this is the time of everything's done by hand, especially the cutting of the patterns in the clothe.

During this time there were not cutting machine. So, you have your pattern, you make your patterns, you put your pattern down, you then draw it out, and then with big scissors, you cut it out. Mrs. Coltrane patiently showed me how to trace out the pattern and then cut it. For me as a young child, this was a big deal. I'm making stuff! I felt was very big, competent, and very proud of myself for helping to making the Dashiki's.

My connection to Mrs. Coltrane has last a lifetime as to this day I remembered her vividly and fondly. The way she gave her time, patience and love helped me to feel that I too can make clothes! Although she was busy working, she gave me her full presence and attention. She believed in me, taught me, and allowed me to be fully engaged, even at 5-year-old!

What struck me most about Miss Coltrane was her kindness. Despite her busy life, she always took the time to engage with me, a young girl who had nothing of tangible value to offer. Yet, she made me feel valued and included in her work. Even as a child, I sensed that there was something special about her.

Most people knew Mrs. Coltrane as a Jazz pianist, a wife, a mother, person who is one dimensional. Yet, she was a full dynamic multi-talented, and exceptional person. Most of us are known as one-dimensional. Most of us are not known at all. Perhaps this is the reason that many of us keep missing each other's humanity because to understand humanity, and to recognize humanity in other people, we must recognize people as multi-dimensional and see them as full people, like ourselves.

Mrs. Coltrane involved me in the process of creating. She valued me and engaged. She was just different. I understood I was making shirts and a creative person. I was making Dashiki's, and I was capable helping to make Dakshiki and she gave me full engagement, patience, and value.

The depth of the time with Mrs. Coltrane. Her way to engagement and the involvement me, was a gift to me. That's amazing. So that really gives you an understanding of what kind of effect do we have on each other, and who do we influence, and will that effect be a positive one that will spread forward 50 years from now, or will it be an effect that's not positive 50 years from now.

Looking back, I realize that Miss Coltrane taught me that humanity is value of yourself, so that you can see it in others, no matter how young. She values of me taught me lessons about kindness and inclusivity. She encouraged me to values myself. She showed me that regardless of our circumstances or background, we can always find ways to uplift and inspire others through showing their value. Her memory has stayed with me all these years, a testament to the profound impact she had on my life.

Alice Lucille Coltrane, Aka Swamini Turiyasangitananda

SECTION II

IF I AM ONLY FOR MYSELF, WHAT AM I?

Humanity Connection – Civility, Respect, Championing

Chapter Five: Cultivating Civility
HRH The Princess Royal - England

Chapter Six: The Power of Respect
Dr Maya Angelou, USA

Chapter Seven: Championing
Ambassador Alfonso Lenhardt, USA

Chapter Eight: Opportunity
Ambassador Henry Owen, USA

Chapter Nine: Forgiveness
Archbishop Desmond Tutu, South Africa

Chapter Ten: Compassion
Pope Francis, Vatican

5

Humanity is Civility

HRH The Princess Royal, United Kingdom

On a typical day at the United Nations Representative, as the Founder and President of Ariel Foundation International, a colleague asked me to accompany her to a meeting at a nearby Wilson Hotel next to the League of Nations (the Petit Palais, the first UN Building). I sat with her at the meeting and listened. I didn't say anything, because it was not my conversation, and I had not been invited to give my thoughts or opinions. With no expectation and very surprised that the gentleman looked up at me. I didn't know him. Mr. John Morrison, said, "tell me what you think" as they were talking about a charity called Acid Survivors Trust International (ASTI) and how they can work with the United Nations as a Non-Governmental Organization (NGO.) ASTI is an organization that would help those who have faced acid violence and the consequences of being burned by acid, usually thrown in their face or on their body. It would cause blindness, the face to melt, and other serious burns that would necessitate many surgeries only to regain function.

Mr. Morrison asked me my opinion about some issues that had to do with policy and working within the United Nations structure. I gave him my opinion and thought that was the end of our association. Later he contacted me and asked me to meet with him and the other Trustee as he wanted to set up some international linkages and structures for ASTI. I was asked to be a Trustee.

After I became a Trustee for the Acid Survivors Trust International, I learned that our charity patron was HRH The Princess Royal. She supported the charity personally and would not only attend by encourage support of ASTI. I had the privilege of meeting Princess Royal twice. Both times were at charity events for ASTI being held at Embassy of Nepal and the Embassy of Pakistan in London.

The first meeting took place at the Nepalese Embassy in London, where ASTI was hosting a charity event to raise funds for survivors of acid attacks. As I mingled with guests, I found myself pleasantly surprised when HRH The Princess Royal approached me directly. Despite the presence of distinguished individuals, she took the time to engage in conversation, displaying a genuine interest in ASTI's mission and the work we were doing. What struck me most was her sincerity and depth of knowledge on the issues of acid violence and the challenges faced by survivors.

Both times the charity event for ASTI was to raise funds, especially for those who needed reconstructive surgery because sometime the acid would cause the Sometimes the nose doesn't work, they can't breathe, they can't eat, it's horrible. They can't see. The Acid violence victims usually need many specialised surgeries.

The second time I met HRH The Princess Royal I was quite surprised, because she was welcomed by the Ambassador from India to the United Kingdom and various of officials that protocol demanded. I did not think that HRH The Princess Royal was going to come to me because there were a lot of very influential and important people in the room. I did not consider myself one of them. And when I say important people, I mean the ambassadors of various countries, high level military and government official and of course those who were quite wealthy, and then there's me. I'm just a Trustee for ASTI, at least in my own opinion, not very important. Not in any way. I was actually very surprised I was standing over in the corner, where I could watch various interactions.

I remember I was standing in the corner. I was very surprised when she came directly to me. Very surprised. Because you had all these other people that she was talking to. And I must be honest, I don't remember the exact conversation we had. Yet, I know she was very curious about the statistics of Acid Violence towards women and its public health implications. Somehow HRH The Princess Royal knew that I was an international public health and policy specialist (PhD from the London School of Hygiene & Tropical Medicine). She asked me about issues for Acid survivors in my expertise.

While speaking with The Princess Royal, I remember thinking, "she is the daughter of the Queen who treats me with such unusual civility and interest." It allowed me to know that there was no seen hierarchy, but we were in this fight for this cause together. HRH The Princess Royal took her time to thoroughly engage with spend time with Acid Survivors Trust International our Trustees, donors, acid survivors and me.

Acid Survivors Trust International
Rebuilding Lives • Stopping Acid Violence

requests the pleasure of the company of

Dr Ariel King

at a reception and buffet dinner to launch the
Burns Violence Survivors-Nepal (BVS-N) organisation
at
The Embassy of Nepal, London
Hosted by His Excellency Dr Suresh Chandra Chalise, Ambassador to the UK
and in the presence of
Her Royal Highness the Princess Royal
Patron of the Acid Survivors Trust International

Wednesday, 6th October 2010, 6.15 - 9.30pm
Embassy of Nepal, 12A Kensington Palace Gardens, London, W8 4QU

RSVP:
Alison Marston: office@asti.org.uk
Tel: 0207 821 1567

Dress:
Lounge Suit/Equivalent for Ladies/
National Dress

Invitation made from Nepalese paper for Acid Survivors Trust Reception with Princess Royal

To my surprise HRH The Princess Royal, even with her hundreds of charities and very full schedule she was fully committed to support that Acid Survivors Trust International. Princess Royal to support ASTI not just in name, but to fully engaged with all its workings, and actively a part of the fundraisers. More importantly, she took the time to know about us as people and Trustees, and those we serve.

HRH The Princess Royal actions truly caught me by surprise because she spent a lot of time, energy, and efforts to help with charities, and gain the support they need to be of service. HRH

The Princess Royal could support charities, like ASTI in name only. Yet she chose to spend hours making our two events a success.

The Second time I met HRH The Princess Royal was for an ASTI fundraiser at the Pakistan Embassy in London. it was small societies' who's who that included diplomats, wealthy businesspeople, celebrities, and special guests, we were no more than 35, 40 people. It was a small reception.

During our brief interaction, HRH The Princess Royal's civility and humility, with a dedication to understanding the complexities of our cause left a lasting impression on me. She wasn't there for a mere photo opportunity; she genuinely wanted to connect with those involved in the charity's efforts, including Trustees like me.

During this reception, once again I had the opportunity to speak with HRH The Princess Royal. Now for the second fundraiser our discussion revealed her deep thinking and the about Acid Survivors and their opportunities for surgeries and psychological support to repair their lives. I was impressed by her breath of knowledge and information about the issues of violence, not just against not just women.

This small reception had many guests who were men. We were separated into small groups during the reception to speak with HRH Princess Royal. In my group, I was the only woman.

HRH The Princess Royal came up to the group and we spoke to her within the group rather than individually. During our time with her I noticed her flat shoes. Then I understood that she was there for the business of raising funds.

Princess Royal looked like she was there to work, and to make the goals for the fundraise happen. But the second I was really impressed because once again, because as a Trustee, we don't know if she's coming or not. We know that she's a patron, so she's a part of the fundraiser. Yet, being physically present was not required.

I was so impressed by HRH The Princess Royal determination. She was there for genuine support, and not just a public relations opportunity. Her concern and support were genuine. I found that hopeful. It made me feel hopeful for humanity. She is someone who was bought up in the British Royal family with all the trappings of wealth, privilege, and protocol, who is committed to victims of acid violence.

HRH Princess Ann and Dr. Ariel Rosita King at the launch of ASTI's Burns Violence Survivors- Nepal at Royal Nepalese Embassy in London, June 2010

The fact that HRH The Princess Royal physically came for a charity event and to loan not just her name, but her physical support to say, I'm here with people who have experienced violence, acid violence." It's not even one of the nice charities, that everyone supports, funds for children, art, or animals. This is the charity that specifically deals with violence, disfigurement, loss and sometimes death. For HRH Princess Royal to come out and say and show "I stand with those who are affected by it, and those who want to help with it, and I'm here to support it." That's amazing.

HRH The Princess Royal is a person with compassion and substance. I'm very impressed by her civility, humility, and her willingness to immerse herself in the work of ASTI, despite her royal status and demanding schedule, as it spoke volumes about her character. She eschewed the trappings of privilege and instead chose to stand in solidarity with those affected by violence, lending her voice and support to a cause that often goes unnoticed.

In a world where appearances often overshadow substance, HRH The Princess Royal's genuine civility, humility with compassion and involvement serves as a beacon of hope. Her actions remind us that true philanthropy requires more than just a name; it demands active engagement and a genuine desire to effect positive change.

As I reflect on these encounters, I am filled with admiration for HRH The Princess Royal and her unwavering commitment to making a difference in the lives of others. Her example serves as a powerful reminder that true greatness lies not in titles or accolades, but in the impact, we have on those around us, that starts and ends with civility.

6

Humanity is Respect

Dr. Maya Angelou

Our family home had an extensive library. Dr Maya Angelou's book, "I Know Why the Caged Birds Sing" with an orange cover, and a black bird was captivating. I took it from our library and started to read it. As an 11-year-old reading the book I was shocked at its honesty and the life experiences that she had as a child and had the honesty and courage to write. My mother, Dr. Margo King, said that she bought the book after Dr Angelou went to speak at her university in New York City.

Many years later as a young student at the University of Hawaii in Manoa, I learned that Dr Angelou was a speaker only minutes away from our campus at a local universal church. I had classes, but I had to go to see the same amazing woman that my mother saw when she was in college at my age. I remember that encounter vividly, as if it happened just yesterday. Meeting Dr. Maya Angelou was more than just a chance encounter; it was a transformative experience that left an indelible mark on me.

The church was filled with excited people. I could feel the specialness of what was to happen in the air through the buzzing of the conversation, laughter, and good will. I looked for a seat in the back. There were no seats left. Yet, seats were added on the left side of the stage on side of the podium where Dr Angelou was to speak. As a person who did not like to sit for long, and to have the freedom to move around and walk around even in my university classes, I had to decide to suspend my personal habit of always being in motion.

I found myself on stage with Dr. Maya Angelou and a handful of others. Mesmerised for hours, she drew me in and enveloped me in her warmth and generosity of spirit. She didn't just speak to us; she provided a space, and a sacred place of acceptance in her presence.

Dr Maya Angelou captivated the audience with her deep voice and profound wisdom as she weaved stories, parable, lessons, and songs that resonated deeply within me. Dr Angelou did not give a speech. Instead, she took us on a journey through time and space, connecting us to our past, present, and future in ways I had never experienced or imagined.

For the first time in my life, I was totally captivated and mesmerized in a time and space that was rare and semi-holy. As she spoke, I felt as though I was part of something sacred, something eternal. It was a feeling unlike anything I had ever experienced before. The experience stayed with me my entire life, long after her presentation about love, life, loss, and humanity had officially ended with applause in which I woke up from the most encompassing dream like state, to give a standing ovation.

As it was time for another class, I went back to school withing minutes on my moped. When the class was over, I decided to go back to the reception for Dr Angelou.

Surprisingly we had a face-to-face encounter. I arrived back at the venue on my moped, I saw Dr Maya Angelou in the back of a car. I waved goodbye to her, and to my surprise, she had the car stopped, and rolled down her window. She asked if she could help me with something, but all I could say was, "Thank you, you've already given me everything."

As I went home and lay in bed thinking that evening about the gifts of life, love and understanding Dr Angelou gave me in one evening. I knew she gave me all her open spirit had to give in such a short intensive time. I was pre-occupied of thinking about how could I give her a little of myself to say "thank you" for what she gave me? I was driven and compelled to express my gratitude in some way. I knew many people and found a friend I knew, who had known the organisers of the event. I called him and asked if he knew someone who could give Dr Angelou a tape of my original 8 song professional album, called "Ariel" that was recorded at Rondez-Vous Studios in Waikiki. The one song, I wanted to dedicate to her was "JonAriel: Teach me to live one day at a time."

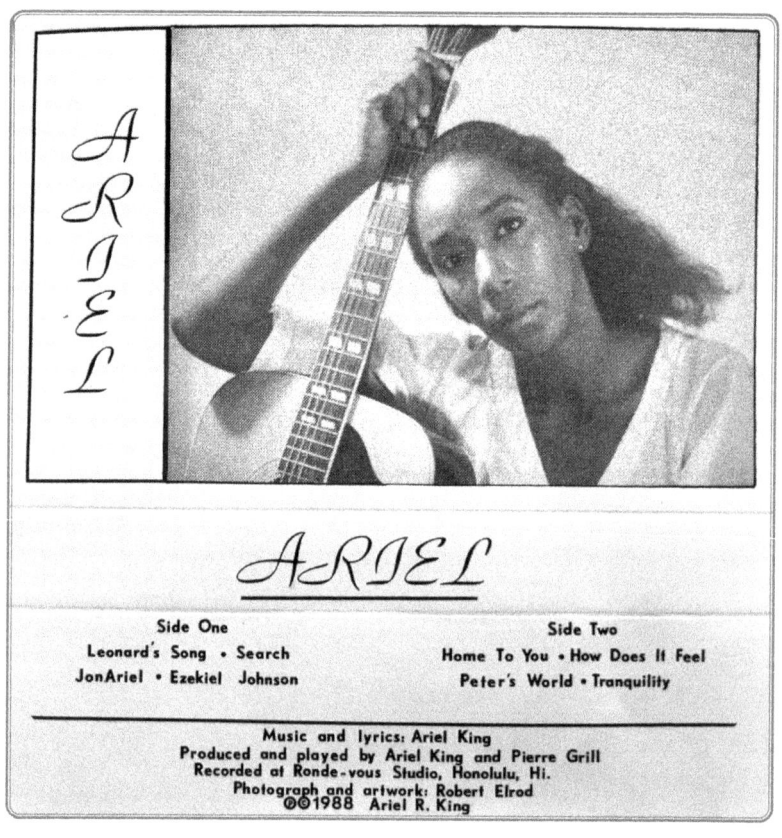

JONARIEL: TEACH ME TO LIVE ONE DAY AT A TIME
Words, music, and recording by Ariel Rosita King ©

I lye still at night, and look up at the stars shining bright,
Saying hello to me, while setting my soul free.
Walking on the sandy beach and loving the message that you teach,
Live, love and laugh today, because tomorrow is so far away.
Teach me to live one day at a time
with courage, love, and a sense of pride.
Giving me that ability to love, and accept myself,
So, I can go and give it to someone else.
Feeling your warmth hold me tight and
letting me know that feeling good is alright.
Cradling me in your arms of love, and letting me know
That I am precious as the stars above.
Teach me to live one day at a time
with courage, love, and a sense of pride.
Giving me that ability to love, and accept myself,
So, I can go and give it to someone else.
Teach me to live one day at a time!

I asked my friend if he could help me give Dr Maya Angelou a gift to show my deepest appreciation. I received a call back that night telling me to go to an address in Waikiki the next day and give the item to a person, with only a first name.

The next day I drove my moped to the address given. It was a tropical small hotel. I waited in the lobby and was picked up by a European looking woman in her 30-40s. She asked me to follow her. I had no idea where I was going, but I followed. We arrived at a brown door on the right. She opened the door, and we walked inside. To my utter shock I was standing in front of me the very tall Dr. Maya Angelou! Enormous smile stretched by lips and my eyes sparkled as I realised that the universe sent me another gift in less than 24 hours! Dr Angelo was in relaxed flowing clothes and her mood was serene as if she had just come back from a meditation session.

Ariel Rosita King on Waikiki Beach, Hawaii

Dr Angelou welcomed me as if I were a young relative. She asked where I wanted to sit inside or outside and gave me refreshments to drink. I was so very happy and chose outside.

Dr Angelou, a remarkable woman, who had already given me so much, graciously accepted my humble offering. Excited I gave her a cassette tape, "of my original folk music titled "ARIEL" that was deeply personal for me, and a letter. She started to read my letter.

The letter read, "Dear Maya"….. Immediately, Dr Angelou said, "Baby, you cannot call me 'Maya'! You can call me Dr Angelo or call me Auntie Maya, or you can call me Dr Maya, but you cannot call me by my first name because we are not friends. I am your elder." I said, Dr Angelou, I would never call you by your first name. She said, "Yes, but you wrote it!" Then I understood for the first time that speaking and writing must be aligned. I apologised.

Dr Angelou wanted to know all about me. She asked me about my family, my subject of study, my life in Hawaii, what profession I was interested. and other questions to get to know me as a unique, and interesting person. I was only in my early 20s, she showed me that I was interesting, important, and worth spending her time only hours after an exhausting performance and reception. After more than an hour of talking on the terrace, Dr Angelou graciously walked me towards the front door of her hotel-apartment. She asked me if I had any other questions. I said, yes. "How do you handle fame, and everyone wanting everything from you, and after you give them all you have, they ask for more?" Dr. Angelou said, "KISS, Keep It Simple, Sweetie."

The opportunity to personally meet and have time with Dr. Maya Angelou, in Hawaii, years after reading her book from our home library, that my mother bought home as a student who also heard her speak in New York at her university was a special life experience. Unexpectantly, being at her presentation, speaking with her on the way out of the reception leaving for the evening, and having a full hour of talking at her apartment hotel, felt like a full-circle fate life experience.

More than ten years later, once again I was in the audience where Dr Maya Angelou was the main speaker for the Annual National Black MBA Association meeting in the US.

Reflecting on that experience now, I realise how fortunate I was to have crossed paths with Dr. Maya Angelou. She taught me valuable lessons about the power of respect, generosity of spirit, and the importance of giving back. Dr Maya Angelou taught me that my humanity requires to both give and receive respect. Thus, I am a better human being than I was before we met.

Composite photos of Dr Maya Angelou

7

Humanity is Championing

H. E. Ambassador Alfonso E. Lenhardt, USA

Ambassador Alfonso E. Lenhardt has championed me in my personal and professional development, which has led to the concept, development and now 24 years old not for profit called Ariel Foundation International, that has passed on the gift of championing children and youth worldwide.

His Excellency, Ambassador Alfonso E. Lenhardt and I met while in a business class lounge in Lanai, Hawaii. We were the only people in the lounge waiting for our local flight to Honolulu. He and his wife were coming back from a holiday. Ambassador Lenhardt was listening to this new age music by the artist "Enya". I said to myself, "This music is a little strange." And I thought, "Well, what kind of music is this? It's not jazz, it's not blues, it's not rock. It is just like new age music." We started to talk about the music. He said that he now enjoyed the music of "Enya", an Irish musician, composer, and singer. He said that he was retired from the military as a general and has lived all over the world with his wife and three daughters.

Our conversation with Mrs. Lenhardt and Ambassador Lenhardt was just fantastic, flowing, and we talked about different places that they've traveled and how they raised their daughters internationally as global citizens. His and his family lived all over the world. Ambassador Lenhardt was one of the highest-ranking military people, as a General of African descent. The time in the lounge went by too fast. Mrs. Lenhardt was also so very engaging and told entertaining stories about their family's international adventures. We all thought there was a connection that we wanted to keep after our brief time together. We exchanged contact information and parted ways to board our different flights.

I lived in Europe. I had planned a trip to the USA and the Washington, DC area. I was looking forward to seeing Ambassador Lenhardt and his wife again. I contacted him while he was the CEO of the Corporate Council on Africa. We would meet and go out to lunch. During this time Ambassador Lenhardt became my mentor. At lunch, we talked about ideas, and I found him inspirational. Once back in Europe we kept in touch by email until I traveled back to the USA. A year or so later when I travelled back to the US to visit family, Ambassador Lenhardt invited me to meet him on Capital hill at the United States Senate. Ambassador Lenhardt was confirmed as the Sergeant at Arms for the United States Senate.

Once again, as he did in the Military, he made history by being the first Sargent at Arms of African American and Caribbean Descent. As the Sargent at Arms, he was the only person in the world who had the authority to arrest a sitting US President! Only days before 11 September 2000 he had just taken up the post as Sargent at Arms.

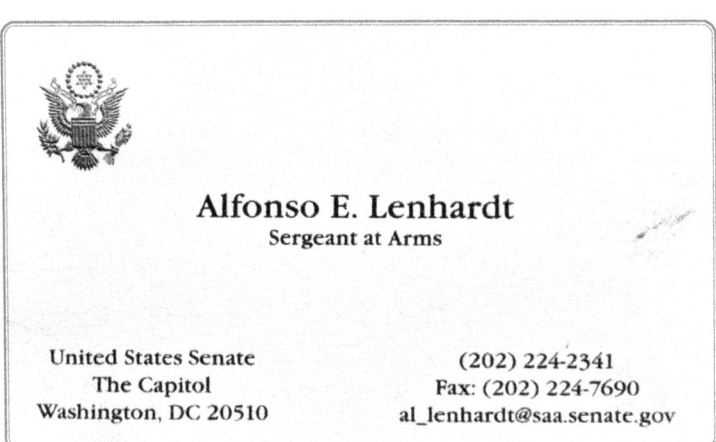

Ambassador Lenhardt, after only days in his new position of Sargent of Arms, there was the attacks of 11 September 2000

(known as 9/11). Just imagine taking on a new position as Sergeant at Arms. He was responsible for the security of the Senate, all the mail, all the communications, and a lot of the special police force. Ambassador Lenhardt even with all these responsibilities, he kept in touch with me.

Ambassador Lenhardt invited me to visit him at his new job. Once we set a date in his calendar, and gave all the official protocol needed, He welcomed me at the Senate Building in Washington, DC. After meeting in his office and taking official photos, Ambassador Lenhardt personally, gave me a tour round of the Senate and introduced me to various people. As a special gift, he also took me to the usually closed, first and oldest Senate Chambers. It was just fantastic. He helped me to experience first-hand how the Senate and its representatives keep the country functioning. I just felt special, because Ambassador Lendhardt gave me his time, energy, and a VIP tour of the Senate of the United States of America.

H.E. Alfonso E. Lenhardt, Sargent at Arm and Ariel Rosita in Original Senate Chambers

Let me tell you the reason that he's also important to me. Over the years we had several informal meetings. We would go to lunch when I was in town. At one lunch, we started talking about his daughters and what they were doing professionally. One of his daughters was a lawyer. And he said to me, "…"she started a foundation." "Pardon?" I said, believing that I did not hear him correctly. "She started a foundation." Now I understood that this was a possibility for my life too! All my life since I had my first event as a pre-teen for raising awareness and funds for Muscular Dystrophy, I have participated in or organised functions to help others. It was and continues to be my calling.

I asked him questions about his daughter and the foundation she started. I was amazed and inspired! Once I realised that it was an option, another world of possibilities opened up for me. I said, "Oh, but you can do that?" Ambassador Lenhardt encouraged me, "Well, yes, if you really think that you want to do it. I think you should try it. There might be some things you have to learn or do ... " Ambassador Lenhardt was encouraging. He did not say, "No, you cannot start a foundation. He said, "Yes, if you'd really think you'd like to do that, I'm sure that you can. You must put some things in order. But I think you'd be very good at it." Ambassador Lenhardt not only encouraged me, but he actively championed me to start my own foundation. I started Ariel Foundation International in December 2000, and receive its charity tax-free legal status in 2002.

After Ambassador Lenhardt left the position of Sergeant at Arms, of the United States Senate, he went on to be President of the National Crime Prevention Council (NCPC). When I called to ask for time with him, once again he made time to meet me at his office. In the following years he served as a diplomat, the United States Ambassador to Tanzania.

I learned several important life lessons from Ambassador Lenhardt. Ambassador Lenhardt was a gentleman, who had tremendous responsibilities for the country and pressure on his time. As a sergeant at arms of the United States Senate, he had no time, but he made time. He never made me feel as if I was rushed or was taking up valuable time. He never gave me the impression or feeling that he did not have time for me. Whenever I was with him, he always allowed me to feel as if he had all the time in the world. Even though he had three successful daughters, and a wonderful wife and an ominous responsibility, when we met, I was the most important person. My importance was inherent in his championing me and my goals.

For someone like me that didn't have VIP credentials, he gave me time and energy as if I were and made me believe that not only am I a VIP, not only am I a very important person, but I have the ability and the capacity to start and run and foundation for children and youth. As a result, of Ambassador Lenhardt's championing, I started Ariel Foundation International in 2000 and it is celebrating a quarter of a century of inspiring leadership, entrepreneurship and community service for children and youth worldwide next year, 2025.

Ambassador Lenhardt is the one major influential person that made the dream become a reality through his championing me throughout my young personal and professional development. He showed me humanity through championing me.

Humanity is Opportunity

H.E. Ambassador Henry David Owen - USA

Our initial connection, H.E. Ambassador Henry David Owen and me was facilitated through mutual acquaintances in Washington, D.C., where I was a member of the Washington, DC Rotary Club. Ambassador Owen was a quiet yet, powerful esteemed figure in international world economic and finance circles.

Sometimes he would talk to me about religion because he was Catholic, and economic institutions like Bretton woods. I told him that I have always wanted to attend the World Economic Forum. To my complete surprise Mr. Owens said, " Schwab and I are friends. We started the World Economic Forum together. " I was simultaneously stunned and impressed. I told Ambassador Owen, "I would like to go and participate. Please can you talk with him?" He said, "Yes".

Ambassador Owen took an interest in speaking with me about youth and the best way to support and mentor them for academic and life success. Although in his 80's, he was quite aware of the pressing societal issues, particularly those related to education and opportunity to support and motivate youth of various cultural backgrounds.

The initiative that Ambassador Owen developed was an NGO then called, his initiatives, Capital Partners for Education (CPE). Since its inception, it has been renamed "Spark the Journey" in 2020. The organization, provides direct one on one mentorship, and financial tuition assistance for private schools to promising students from underserved communities, enabling them to access quality private education opportunities.

Ambassador Owen's passion for empowering young people was evident in every discussion we had. He emphasized the importance of providing resources and guidance to help students realise their full potential, regardless of their socioeconomic background. Through his efforts, he sought to give equal financial and mentor support to create pathways for success for those facing economic and social challenges in the USA.

As our relationship evolved, I had the privilege of serving as a mentor within the Capitol Partners for Education program, supporting students as they navigated the transition to private school education. Additionally, I collaborated with Ambassador Owen on various programming initiatives aimed at expanding access to educational and cultural opportunities and promoting diversity in mentorship.

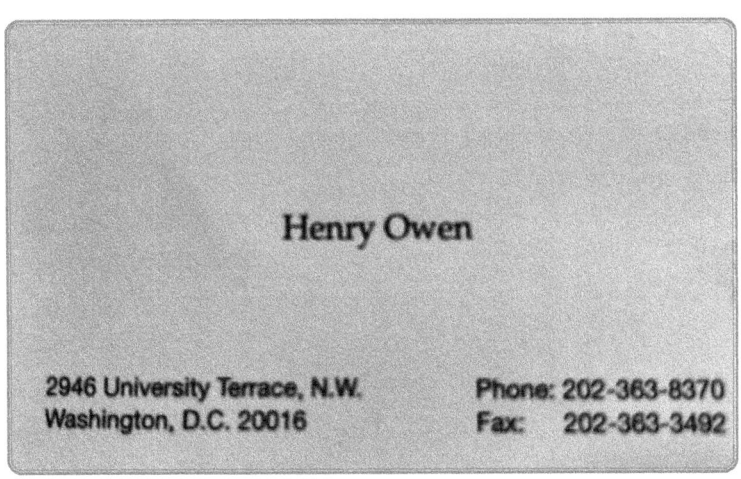

Business card, simple and understated from Ambassador Henry Owen

We had many lunches together at the private Metropolitan Club. We talked about life, our families, and our belief in doing good. We also talked about US economics, my experiences, and views about youth opportunities. He would talk with me about the United States economic structure, and how it affects the education and opportunities for young people. Also, the ways in which young people need to traverse or go beyond some of the limiting issues of economy and economics, especially when they're not born into wealthy families, to access privileged resources, especially private high school education. Many of the private schools in Washington, DC had a tuition of a minimum of $20,000 dollars per year in the early 2000s.

The most important impression from Ambassador Owen was his genuine commitment to making a difference in the lives of young people. Despite privilege and societal position, and his advanced age, he remained deeply invested in the cause, actively engaging with mentors and mentees to ensure the success of the program through various opportunities for young people.

Celebrating 15 Years of Making College Possible

Our discussions extended beyond education to encompass broader economic issues, religious, societal, and philosophical debates. Ambassador Owen's Curiosity, intellectual stimulation, and appreciated the diverse perspectives I brought to our conversations, which spanned topics ranging from global economics to personal philosophies.

Ambassador Owen was active at 91 years old with Capital Partners on Education until he passed away in 2011. Today Mr. Schwab and Mr. Kahari Brown remain at the former Capital Partners for Education, now called "Spark the Journey". Also, the focus is now on helping academic middle grade achieving high school students and first in the family college students to gain admissions, remain and graduate from college with the support and assistance of a mentor and the collective supportive program.

Looking back, I am grateful to have crossed paths with Ambassador Henry David Owen. Although he sought my humble advice, professional friendship, and me as a mentor for a youth in his program, he was also a special mentor and supporter for me and my professional aspirations.

His legacy serves as a testament to the power of opportunity through mentorship, education, and advocacy in working together to bring about a better future on young person at a time. Though our lunch meetings and Capital Partner Education meetings were for serval years, the impact of his vision and mentorship continues to resonate, inspiring me to work for positive change for youth in my own sphere of influence to give children and youth opportunities to better themselves, their communities, and the world at large.

H.E Ambassador Henry David Owen

9

Humanity is Forgiveness

Archbishop Desmond Tutu – South Africa

The Institute of Shipboard education was having a Semester at Sea "alumni cruise". In September 1982, I went literally around the world to 13 countries for the first time.

Knowing that Lesotho is landlocked and surrounded by South Africa, the ocean was far away. I decided to ask H.E. Ambassador Molelekeng Ernestina Rapolaki; (Ambassador to the USA from the Kingdom of Lesotho), and her oldest son to be my guests along with my husband, grandmother, and oldest daughter, Ariana-Leilani. When I formally introduced H. E. Ambassador Molelekeng Ernestina Rapolaki to Archbishop Tutu, I learned that they had known each other in Lesotho. He was a professor at the university in the Kingdom of Lesotho when he left South Africa under apartheid. I had no idea.

During the alumni trip one of the passengers and the special speaker was Archbishop Desmond Tutu. On the day of the talk most families sent their children to a child's function. The staff said, "Well, why don't you let your children go to another room and watch a movie?" And I thought, "No, I think it's better for her to be here to see and hear Archbishop Tutu" As an international child, Ariana-Leilani has been on many international trips with me. She was called the "Little Ambassador" for most of her childhood.

As usual, I actively allowed my daughter to experience people, places, lectures, etc. in various countries with a lot of different leaders. Now, when I look back at the photos and see that she was in constant movement on the floor, and doing what active three-year-old's do! She was on the floor, she has an arm up, feet up, she is up and down. Yet, it was right next to Archbishop Desmond Tutu. He was very calm and very nonchalant. It was almost as if it was one of his grandchildren. Just another grandchild in front of him while he was talking to guests.

At the end of his talk, he stood up, and Ariana-Leilani stood up too. She ran and jumped into his arms! He caught her! Their communication without words was special. Amazed, I took a picture of Archbishop Tutu catching Ariana-Leilani.

After that special day, what really surprised me is Ariana-Leilani for days did not see Archbishop Tutu. Yet, each day Ariana-Leilani would literally say, "Where is Uncle?" "I'm going to find Uncle." After several days, when she finally found him, on the ship, she happily shouted, "I found Uncle. I found him! I found Uncle!"

The second time, we engaged with Archbishop Tutu on the ship was a little more formal because he was under a lot of pressure of time and expectations. People were lined up to speak with him and get books and other items signed. I had Ariana-Leilani stand in line with a book that was written by him to be gifted to Ambassador Rapolaki. I gave this book to Ariana-Leilani, even though she was three, to have it signed by Archbishop Desmond Tutu, to give it to Ambassador Ropolaki, who's is still with our foundation today, 18 -years later! I have a picture of Ariana-Leilani having the book signed. It was interesting is he didn't treat her any differently than he would've treated Ambassador Rapolaki. He sat there with Ariana-Leilani, gently and carefully took the book she handed to him. He said, "Would you like me to sign it here?" She was fully engaged in the task and gave him the spot to sign. He complied!

Archbishop Tutu had a full and unabandoned laughed as if he had been to the deepest deaths of despair and learned to forgive. Archbishop Tutu showed strong resiliency, like a bouncing ball. The harder you bounce it down, the higher it will rise. In the depths of despair through forgiveness reaps laughter and joy. This is the first lesson on Humanity I learned from Archbishop Tutu. The second lesson of Humanity I learned is that it is important to have compassion for, and whenever possible to forgive people. His compassion made all the difference when he used it to enhance his ability to forgive those who participated in horrific inhumane actions in apartheid South Africa that are unforgiveable.

Archbishop Desmond Tutu, a noble peace prize winner, found value in everyone. He was the Chair of the Truth and Reconciliation Committee for the new South after apartheid. He said that during some of the testimonies he felt despair and deep sadness. Archbishop Tutu knows the depth of despair and the height of joy of life through compassion and ultimate forgiveness.

Humanity is Forgiveness 91

Archbishop Desmond Tutu catches Ariana-Leilani, and Dr King on Semester at Sea ship

Ariana-Leilani Hugging "Uncle" Archbishop Desmond Tutu

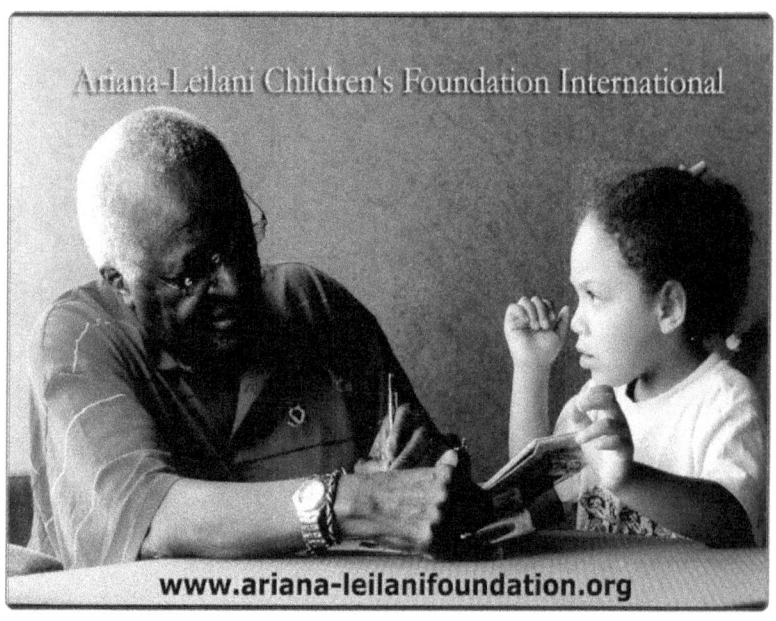

Ariana-Leilani Children's Foundation teaching and advocating for children's rights.

10

Humanity is Compassion

Pope Francis – Vatican

As an active organiser, partner, and supporter of "The Road to Change" for Awareness about child sexual abuse. The two-year walking tour to twenty-eight countries in the European Union by my colleague and friend, Dr Matthew McVarish. The Road to Change tour was to bring awareness, education and encourage active discussion and legislation on child sexual abuse. Road to Change allowed us to be to meet with Pope Francis at the Vatican in Italy.

We arrived in the city of the Vatican in the late evening. I had organised our accommodation so that we would be walking distance to the Vatican since we had to be there extremely early, even with a personal invitation. Very early in the morning about 5:00 am we woke up and readied for our day at the Vatican. We did not have breakfast as we were too nervous and excited. We arrived at Vatican gates of the specific church on the at about 6:00am. To my surprise there were thousands of people that had invitations to go through various entrances. The entrance was specified on our invitation. There was a buzz of excitement in the air. Almost as if we were at a popular outdoor music concert with very rare tickets for entry. After waiting only a short time, the doors opened.

To my shock, nuns in their full nun habits and uniforms and head coverings ran so very fast, that I was sure they had been on track team and football teams! Not only did they run fast, but they actively pushed anyone and everyone out of their way to get through the door first. Since we had a special invitation, we were taken through a much less crowded entry by the elite Swiss security who wore special red suits.

We were taken through a hallway and a special door that when we entered the church we were in the front of the church and looking back was three sections of a "small church" that held several thousand people. We were in the very first front row of single chairs and about the 4th and 5th people from the left.

The people filled the church. They were chanting and singing in various languages, I especially took note of those from African countries singing in melodic African languages and meter as it freed the mind and called to the body to move to its melodious beat. The entire building was enveloped in a beautiful full sound.

No less than eight bishops help to carry out the service. Pope Francis sat on the stage on a large white chair. Prayers were conducted in Latin, and some blessings in Spanish and Italian.

After the religious service Pope Francis came to the first row with a host of other people, his assistants, bishops, photographers, and videographer. We were in the very first row. The two rows behind us were couples who had married and came to receive a special blessing. Behind them was a separation and another 6-7 rows of people, and behind the third row was thousands of people, many who stood up from their seats to be an active part of the service.

I stood in front of the sixth seat in a line to meet Pope Francis. It wasn't an ordinary encounter. It was a moment charged with electric energy and a calm charisma, even for someone like me who is not Catholic, yet spiritual. As he approached me, I was holding a picture of my daughter, Ariana-Leilani, who was about ten years old at the time. I felt a sense of anticipation mixed with a hint of awkwardness and doubt. Would he understand my request for prayers, even though I wasn't part of his faith?

My doubts slipped away as I stood before him, I felt warmth and compassion emanating from Pope Francis, along with charisma. Despite the bustling room, lights of a camera, the priests standing next to him, and the pressures on his time, he looked me directly in the eyes, took my hand, as I showed him Ariana-Leilani's picture and asked for his prayers. In that moment, I felt a connection that transcended religious boundaries. In that moment, there was no one there but Pope Francis and me. I felt true compassion.

What left a strong impression was Pope Francis's genuine compassion and willingness to pause, despite the urging of those around him to move on to the next person. Here was a man of immense influence, yet he took the time to truly see me, hold my hand, ask me questions, and then acknowledge my plea for prayers to help my daughter. It was a gesture that touched me so deeply, it brought comfort to my soul, and almost tears to my eyes.

Reflecting on that encounter now, I realise the profound impact of Pope Francis's humanity. He didn't just offer prayers; he offered his presence, his attention, and his heart. And in doing so, he reminded me of the importance of being fully present for others, regardless of our differences or the pressures we face.

As I look back on that moment, I'm reminded of the power of genuine connection and empathy. Pope Francis exemplified these qualities, showing me that true compassion knows no bounds or limitations.

Pope Francis and Dr Ariel King at the Vatican

Pope Francis and Dr Ariel King requesting prayer for Ariana-Leilani at the Vatican

SECTION III

IF NOT NOW, THEN WHEN?

Humanity Now

Chapter Eleven: Joy
Dr Cornel West, USA and Germany

Chapter Twelve: Connection
Paul Mitchell, Scotland/USA*

Chapter Thirteen: Kindness
Corrine Dettmeijer- Vermuelen, Netherlands

Chapter Fourteen: Humility
President F.W. De Klerk, South Africa

11

Humanity is Joy

Dr. Cornel West – USA

The International World AIDS Conference, Keep the Promise on 22 July 2012 was in Washington, DC. It was finally the first time again, when all people regardless of their HIV status could enter the United States of America. Prior to this a person who was not a US citizen or resident had to be HIV negative to be allowed into America. The outdoor gathering was hosted by Dr Cornel West, Dr Tavis Smiley and Mr. Michael Weinstein, co-founder and CEO for AIDS Healthcare Foundation and the bi-annual International AIDS

Summit, along with former Mayor Andrey Young, Reverend Al Sharpton, Margaret Cho, and the musician Wycelff Jean.

I was sitting on the grass in the audience with thousands of others listening and watching Dr. Cornel West, Tavis Smiley speak, and various people speak for the support of those infected and affected by HIV and AIDS. Although, I was considered one of 50 International world experts on HIV/AIDS, I didn't feel a deep connection to the speakers. I'm watch them, but it's like watching television. Then they said, okay, who would like to volunteer to come up on stage to dance. To be honest, I am a shy person, who loves both privacy and anonymity. I would rather people know my name, but not my face. I know most people won't believe it, but I really am a shy person.

I thought, "I love dancing, but I'm not a dancer on stage, especially in front of thousands of people and cameras in Washington, DC!" The people on stage were in front of 1000s of people, in the audience and thousands more watching as it was a live broadcast. I had decided that my young daughter Ariana-Leilani was a dancer, she loved to dance anywhere, at any time in front of anyone! I know she would have been the first to run onstage to dance if she were there with me.

My commitment to live the life my, in the courageous and loving way daughter would have, allowed me to experience something I would have never experienced. As a shy person I would not volunteer to dance in public in front of so many others. I love dancing, and I love music, but I wouldn't have done it. Yet, standing in the place for my daughter, I felt okay, "I am going to do it. I'm going to live my life right now for her. I am going to volunteer to dance for her, in her place." With newly found courage I got up from the ground and walked towards the back of the stage. To my surprised there was a lot of security.

Once on the stage, the stage manager asked me only my full name; I told him, went to the front stage area, and started to dance with others who volunteered and professional dancers. I didn't expect to dance with anybody specifically. I found myself happily lost in the music and strangely felt calm, as I moved my feet and body to the music and found various dance partners and dance languages. I saw no one in the audience and felt no anxiety. I was fully engaged and present in those moments.

As we danced there was nothing more important than relating to each other and communicating with each other through dance. The dance mirroring while looking at each other allows you to be in another's space and realm just for a short time.

There was a moment in time, where not just the universe stopped, but the universe was dance, the universe was communication through art, through dance, through our spirits. Laughing, playing, engaging and being human. I was in a bubble of bliss with the singer Wycliff, Margaret Cho, professional dancers, audience dancers and some speakers all started to dance together. Time had stood still. As I danced, somehow, I and Dr Cornel West found a dance rhythm together. No one was there but us! There were no longer the people that I saw from the stage, instead, in that moment, there was only us lost in the music and each other, and pure and abandoned joy!

There was a little bubble or a little shield around us including when I was dancing with Dr. Cornel West. No one else existed, and we had the most fantastic time. Dr Cornel West embodied a specialness that comes when someone can make you feel like you're the only one in the room.

After our joyous dance, we hugged. He showed the largest smile with and eyes squinting with joy! I was feeling the same, as if for a moment I experienced the pure abandoned joy of life. Le joie le vie! For those minutes nothing else matters.

Dr. West taught me the beauty of abandoned joy—the kind that blossoms in the moment, unencumbered by worries or distractions. His presence, often associated with intellect and activism, emulated an unexpected warmth, inviting me into a realm of shared humanity.

Looking back, I realize that our dance was more than just a physical expression—it was a celebration of life, love, and the indomitable spirit of humanity. In the midst, of a global crisis, we found solace in the simple act of coming together, united in our pursuit of a brighter tomorrow.

As the event drew to a close, and we parted ways, I carried with me a newfound sense of purpose and possibility. Dr. West had reminded me of the power of joy—the kind that springs from deep within and radiates outward, touching the lives of all who encounter it.

In the days and weeks that followed, I reflected on the lessons learned from that unforgettable encounter. I realized that joy isn't just an emotion—it's a state of being, a choice we make to embrace life fully, despite its challenges and uncertainties.

Dr. West showed me that joy isn't reserved for special occasions or grand gestures—it's found in the everyday moments of connection, kindness, and authenticity. It's a beacon of hope that illuminates even the darkest of days, reminding us that we are all interconnected, bound together by the common thread of our shared humanity.

I carry with me the memory of our dance, a testament to the enduring power of joy and the transformative impact of human connection. In a world often fraught with division and despair, it serves as a reminder that, in the end, joy that will always prevail.

Dr Cornell West and Dr Ariel King hug after dance on stage with musician Wycleff, Margaret Cho at the Washington, DC "Keep the Promise HIV/AIDS Rally.

Humanity is Joy 107

Dr King Marching and advocating for people living with HIV/AIDS

12

Humanity is Connection

Cyril Thomson Mitchell - Scotland

As my life happens, I came back to Honolulu, Hawaii from a summer volunteering at the St Luis Palliative Care Hospital in Jerusalem, Israel at 25 years old. Before I left, I had completed my graduation and ceremony from the University of Hawaii - Manoa. Just before I left for Israel for the summer, I was told that I needed to go back to take one more course to receive my undergraduate degree. Since I did not reserve housing for the upcoming Fall semester, I asked a friend to give my deposit to reserve housing at the University of Hawaii-Manoa for the semester.

I arrived back from two days of travelling from Jerusalem to Honolulu, contacted my friend to find out what university housing I was assigned to, and learned that he did not give the university my deposit, but used it for himself. I was shocked, angry at him for his selfishness, and at a loss because now I had no housing, nowhere to live while my classes were starting in just a week. I went to the housing office to find as I had expected, no available housing and a long waiting list.

While talking to an older university friend about my trip to Israel, I told her about my shock in not having university housing. My friend, said that she would ask her boss, where she was a "vegetarian cook and nanny," if I could stay with her until my university housing was worked out. Her boss said, "yes". On that day I was picked up at the university and bought to a Honolulu compound hidden with large foliage. It's beautiful. It's a very big house. It had swimming pool in the middle of the courtyard with other houses. I had my own little house with a living area, bedroom, bathroom, and small kitchenette. Quickly I settled in and went to take a shower. As I am washing my hair, I see the shampoo and conditioner and think "Oh, nice white with black bottle that reads, 'Paul Mitchell.' Oh, that's interesting. " I continue to wash and condition my hair. I thought nothing of it and I'm just clueless.

Humanity is Connection 111

Ariel Rosita King graduation form University of Hawaii 1987

Later in the evening I was invited to the bigger house for dinner. I still did not know the name of the boss of my friend. I had no idea whose home I was given hospitality. My friend asked, "Well, you do know "Paul Mitchell' products, don't you?" I said, "Who?" "Cyril Mitchell, you're staying at his home!" "Yes. Who?" After many hours at my new hosts home, I still had no idea whose home and from whom I was given such warm hospitality. Days later I learned that my host was Mr. Cyril Thomson Mitchell," the co-founder and co-owner of "Paul Mitchell Professional Hair Systems" and products. "Paul Mitchell" is the combination of his partner John Paul Dejoria and Cyril Thomas Mitchel, uses one name from each for their products "Paul Mitchell".

Cyril Thomson Mitchell, Co-owner of John Paul Mitchell Systems

I didn't get to meet Mr. Mitchell at once. Although I did meet and have time with his teenage son, Angus, who loved music and theater, when we picked him up at the small private school he attended.

After several days at the house. One day my friend said, "Oh, Cyril said, he wants to cut your hair." Stunned I said, "He wants to do what?" She said again, "He wants to cut your hair." Still, I do not know that he is a world-famous hairstylist who has built his family wealth on using natural plants from Hawaii, who is a nature lover, and who's such an unusual man. Mr. Mitchell was innovative and very forward-thinking. So much so, that he had solar energy cars made to race in Australia, that he showed me during the time I was there.

Finally, I said, "Okay" to the haircut. We go back out to the pool. On the left side in a corner there was a little area with a barber seat, with all his hairstyling tools. My chair was turned towards the swimming pool. Mr. Mitchell decided to give me a haircut that goes against tradition. Mr. Mitchell was in his element and was happy combing my hair in various ways to figure out what creative cut he would make. Within a short time, he turned my chair towards the mirror and gave me a mirror to see his creativity. I was happily surprised! Mr. Mitchel cut the back of my hair on a vertical line that was short on the left side and became longer towards the right side. For the first time in my life, I understood personally that creativity is fueled by imagination and openness to try something new. I wore my new vertical cut hair style with amusement and confidence.

Simultaneously, there were several guests at the compound of Mr. Cyril Mitchel. One guest was named, "Milli" she was apartment mates with the model Iman, in New York City. Milli was at least 20 years older than me, kind, sophisticated and interesting.

We had the opportunity to talk and learn a bit about each other and I learned that Milli was amazing and accomplished woman in her own right.

One evening I was invited by Cyril Mitchell, to spend the evening with him, Ms. Milli and his only child, Angus. Angus declined saying, "You old people, I'm not hanging out with you." Angus, stayed upstairs in his room while we three would enjoy the evening together under a cool breeze and the most beautiful night sky filled with clear bright stars.

We sat in a circular furniture in an open-air courtyard with a swimming pool. You can look up at the stars shining clearly and bright. On this night, it was the first time in a long time I felt that all was right on heaven and earth. We were talking openly with each other, we were laughing, I played the guitar, and we all sang. All was right with the world. We were just in an element, our bubble where nobody else existed but us. We were happy, and we understood each other, and there's understanding between us. We were speaking the same non-verbal language through music. But not just music, but also understanding the world around us and appreciating each other and appreciating the world around us.

My friend allowed me to have this contact and connection. She asked for my stay at Mr. Mitchel's home, and it has forever changed my experience and understanding of connection to and for others.

I felt a deep connection with Cyril Mitchell and Milli, and all around me. I was in my true element. I was with people that I understood, and who understood me. I had felt that heaven was on earth in that moment, in that time, all was right with the world; all! I felt a deep humanity in connection.

CYRIL THOMSON MITCHELL 1936-1989

13

Humanity is Kindness

Corrine Dettmeijer- Vermuelen, Netherlands

Rarely do I meet a person who is so accomplished, approachable, personable, kind, and full of the "let us work to make it happen!" as the Honorable Corrine Dettmeijer-Vermuelen. Truth be told, I not only admire her, but also want to actively immolate her positive influence in the lives of others and myself.

Lady Dettmeijer-Vermuelen when we first met in Vilnius, was the Special Rapporteur on Child-Trafficking for the Government of Netherlands. She was a judge, a professor, an important architect of children's rights worldwide, and even the law course to accredit law students in advance children's rights.

We were both speakers for an international organization meeting for children's exploitation and were also two of three international European experts to have official meetings at the Seimas, the Lithuanian Parliament to speak about child trafficking. Immediately we were drawn to each other to learn more about what we were actively pursuing for children.

I told her about a Children's European Human Rights Tour I was planning for children who had the least possibility of a voice. She was intrigued by this idea, unusual and daring. Lady Dettmeijer-Vermuelen invited me to bring the children to see her at the Netherlands Government offices at the Hague. I agreed that a children's human rights tour needed time at the Hague that is so important for international justice, including the International Criminal Court.

Months later, after all the formal arrangement, on the tour with four children and another adult, walked to a large very intimidating official building. The security called up and a young lady brought us upstairs to meet Lady Dettmeijer-Vermuelen. What a special day- It was International Children's

Day! We were brought to a conference room where it was set up for our official meeting.

We, the children and we two adults, were welcomed as if we were important officials. As we sat around the mahogany oblong conference table, Lady Dettmeijer-Vermuelen kindness was apparent in her voice, tone, attention and in providing tea and cookies! She asked each child delegate their opinion of various children's rights issues. The way she spoke to them was filled with respect, consideration, and an expectation to get information that was important for children's rights. The children felt the kindness and it gave them the comfort and confidence to rise to the occasion.

Lady Corrine Dettmeijer-Vermuelen

Although I knew that Lady Dettmeijer-Vermuelen was a champion in front and behind closed doors, I was pleasantly surprised by her official, caring and kindness in handling of the meeting on the same level that she would a group of adults. I remember that the children delegates even received one of her legal publications **on** children's issues. The children delegate felt their importance and rose to the occasion in their interactions.

We as a children's human rights team felt that Lady Dettmeijer-Vermuelen gave us the gift of her kindness and considered the full presence of our children delegates for children's rights. We left the meeting and went out into the brisk air of the Hague with a sense of representation and accomplishment for International Children's Day.

As a mentor, Lady Dettmeijer-Vermuelen, gave me the privilege of meeting with her several times lunch to ask for personal and professional advice. Once again, she was fully present with me, to give me not only her opinions but also paths to meet my goals. There were no interruptions, and I felt heard and understood. Her kindness once again resonated.

As we have met formally twice in Europe, Vilnius, and The Hague, our third formal event was in New York at the United Nations. Through Ariel Foundation International we had a side event on Child Exploitation of which Lady Dettmeijer-Vermuelen was an inspiring speaker.

Her presentation was on the whole child and treatment for children who has been trafficked to cut the psychological, mental, and physical ties from their traffickers. The practical way the programme was designed, implemented, and evaluated was unusual. Once again, I found myself, not only learning from Lady Dettmeijer-Vermuelen, but also wanting to emulate her ability to be kind, clearly and totally presence with me and others regardless of their age and social standing.

Lady Dettmeijer-Vermuelen understood that kindness, brings the best forth from people and situations and allows for the best to come from humanity.

Dr King and Lady Corrine Lady Dettmeijer-Vermuelen, with Ariel Foundation International Children's Human Rights European Tour participants on International Children's Day at her office in the Hague

14

Humanity is Humility

President Frederik Willem De Klerk, South Africa

Enchantingly, for most of my life I had been in long-distance and up close and personal relations with South Africa, its land and its' people in some way. As a teen growing up in a very comfortable New York suburb, reading the book "Cry the Beloved Country" by Allen Paton, and having a South African neighbor, the Taitz family, who left South Africa for a better life for their toddler son, became close family friends for decades. Before I had set foot on the soil of South Africa I had a deep love for the land, and the people because of knowing the Taitz family who showed me the beauty of the country and people at odds with itself.

As an undergraduate student at the University of Hawaii-Manoa, I was a part of the student movement for our university's divestiture and sanctions to bring an end to Apartheid in South Africa. When the Board of Regents finally agreed after a long fight, my joyous reaction was caught in a photo with my fist in the air and my joy apparent. South Africa in its newly formed government and painfully present healing process I believed was on its way to equality. I have had a very intense relationship with the country. I loved South Africa and its people!

As a Rotary Ambassadorial Scholar for academics for two years I was given a large scholarship for my PhD work at University of London, London School of Hygiene and Tropical Medicine. My field research in South Africa was carried out while assigned to the University of Cape Town (UCT). I completed my infield research in 2001.

As an active Rotarian and an alumni, of both, Group Study Exchange (Madagascar) and Ambassadorial Scholar (University of Cape Town, South Africa), I decided to attend the 2011 Rays Rotary Reunion, Rotary Project Expo and Rotary Governors Council of Southern and East Africa four-day reunion in Cape Town. The Rotary International President, Ray Klinginsmith, an

American was also a Rotary exchange Student at the University of Cape Town in 1960 in South Africa and considered it to be one of the most significant influences in his life. Also, Rotarian Bud Kreh was an alumnus in 1950, and I from 1999 to 2001. University of Cape town hosted the reunion of several of us alumni who had over the past 60 years benefited from Rotary International's suite of education grants, notably for its Ambassadorial Scholarships, Group Study Exchange, and Rotary Peace Fellowships programmes.

As a part of our Rotary program, former President Frederik Willem De Klerk, who himself was a Rotarian was an official and announced as guest speaker at our event.

F.W De Klerk was the President of South Africa from 1989 to 1994, and as Deputy President and the last head of State in the era of Apartheid, and Vice President, under President Nelson Mandela after Apartheid, of which the two won the Nobel Peace Prize.

As a person of African descent (Sierra Leone) who has had important connections to South Africa, I was stunned to see President F. W. De Klerk in front of me with only 25 or so other people in the world! I was only several feet away from the former South African FW President who lived in, defended, and gave support to the legal separations of people, opportunities and assets based on melanin colour.

As he stood before us, an ordinary man in blue pants and a dress jacket and shirt and no tie, he looked like an ordinary man, and not the monster I had envisioned when I saw him on television. We were in an ordinary small university auditorium; I sat in the second row almost in front of where he addressed us.

I expected and looked for something horrific to match what I fought against for years; what I thought I knew as evil embodiment in a government represented by one man. Instead, what I experienced was a thoughtful, sensitive, logical, and strategic middle-aged man with a very good sense of humor, and a touch of charisma. He looked directly at me as he spoke and I at him. Although uncomfortable I was intensely interested in what he had to say. Dissonance of what I have thought my whole life with the man in front of me. I saw and experienced a man with humility that was surprising and endearing.

President FW De Klerk, talked about his life, his family, and the change of political thought about the continued viability of apartheid to save himself, his political party, and perhaps share power rather than loose it completely. His political party and he were deeply affected by sanctions, world support for change and near bankruptcy.

He allows us to see inside a man with both conviction and courage, but now to say his was wrong, the system was wrong, and it needed to change for a new South Africa. De Klerks actions from actively changed from defending apartheid to fighting within his government and going against a deeply entrenched system of privilege and discrimination to dismantle it from the inside-out to save his party, save face and perhaps most importantly save himself and his legacy. President FW De Klerk was no saint, or liberator, yet he had courage to negotiate a change. He literally put his own life in danger going against the tides of keeping apartheid in place. As he spoke to us, he never referred to himself as having courage. He talked about his process of thinking, soul searching and then a turnabout to not only accept, but actively help others to come to terms with adapting to the change that held him and his colleagues in splendid privilege, comfort, and wealth for generations.

As President FW D Klerk spoke, I realized that the system of apartheid was not so simple. Bringing apartheid to an end was only possible by those who constructed it, defended it and try to keep it in place could only me dismantled on the inside by the leader of the ruling apartheid political party.

As I listened, daydreamed of the pain of apartheid, and came back to see a humble, and courageous man standing in front of me taking responsibility for his unforgiveable actions, asking for nothing, but giving us everything and showing humility.

President FW De Klerk gave me the gift of understanding that no matter how flawed our actions or thinking, we can change the course of history with humility. Humility allows change to do better while healing deep wounds of an entire nation. Humanity is possible only with humility.

"Rays Rotary Reunion" International at University of Cape Town

Members and beneficiaries (Dr Ariel King upper level in Yellow) from Rotary International programmes gathered at UCT recently to share their experiences, organised by Ray Klingensmith, President of Rotary International, (2011) (Pictures by Roger Sedres.) Source: UCT News.

SECTION IV

IF NOT ME, THEN WHO?

(Dr Ariel KING)

Chapter Fifteen: Compassion
Dr. Elisabeth Kubler-Ross

Chapter Sixteen: Responsibility
Dr Matthew McVarish, Scotland

Chapter Seventeen: Consideration
President Nelson Mandela, South Africa

Chapter Eighteen: Legacy
King Family Legacy Dr. Margo G. King, Ariana-Leilani King-Pfeiffer & Victoria Anya King (USA, and EU)

15

Humanity is Compassion

Dr. Elizabeth Kubler-Ross, Switzerland/ USA

As a young pre-med student just starting out at the university of Hawaii, I had just transferred from Bryn Mawr College, a all-girls college in Pennsylvania. A decision to actively change my life after completing Semester at Sea student trip around the world to thirteen countries in100 days. Now I had to adapt to a new welcomed world of a large public university in a new state, Hawaiian culture and life.

Doing all I could you volunteer, learn from lectures, and join clubs to get to know my new academic home in Hawaii which was so different than the one I had come from. As a volunteer at Kapiolani Children's Hospital I saw a poster for a lecture by Dr Robert Gallo on the HTLV-III Virus (Human T-Cell -Lymphotropic Virus 3), now call HIV Human Immuno Virus, to be given at the Queens Hospital Auditorium in Honolulu.

Dr Robert Gallo was an hour late because he lost his swim trunks in the sea at Waikiki beach while swimming! Dr Gallo was engaging, and I found the subject of this mystery virus to be very interesting. At the lecture I met a nurse who was married to one of the few physicians that work with people with the HTLV-III or HIV Virus. She was the only female helping. We talked about the unknown virus and how it was affecting and killing so many people in Hawaii. Many thought it was only a gay disease. and I had decided that I wanted to help and be a part of helping in any way I could with this new disease. In my early twenties I became a founding member of the Life Foundation of Hawaii (for HIV/AIDS). As the volunteer coordinator I had responsibility for the help hotline and the buddy volunteers that helped and visited those with HIV. As a coordinator I was funded to go to the very last one-week in-residence workshop on "Death, Dying and Transition" with Dr. Elizabeth Kubler-Ross and her assistant outside of Honolulu, Hawaii. The week-long residence workshop attendees were a mix of people: terminally ill, grieving family members, professionals, and those who were living with trauma. The days were intense with various types of experiential therapies, talking groups, exercise activities, artistic expression, and music. We were a small world unto ourselves with no outside disturbances of mobile phone, regular phone, television, or radio. We had nature, the ocean, good organic food, and one another.

As one of the youngest "professional" participants I found the workshops to be incredibly intense. People bore their souls, told their stories, cried warm tears, and beat large thick phone books to pieces. Each of us participants took a turn at talking about our deepest fears, and our lives. Dr Kubler-Ross was there for all the sessions that at times would go for hours several times a day. I found that I had to escape the room of feelings, tears, laughter and at time unleashed joy for life. It seems all too intense for me. One day, Dr Kubler-Ross said that it was now my turn. I was not prepared for opening my emotions to people I did not know , or to show my feelings, my life, traumas or hopes. She gently guided me with basic supportive questions. Before I knew it, I too was crying, releasing my deepest sadness, and using boxes of tissues to blow my nose that was running along with the tears. I was able to find myself through the sadness and disappointments.

The next day it was my turn to go from the experiences that release sadness to that to release anger that I avoided at all costs. Once again in a group setting sitting on the floor with pillows, blankets, and very think 3-4-inch yellow pages (business) telephone books and a 2-inch round rubber hose. At first my hitting of the phone book with the rubber hose seemed contrived. I blocked any feelings of sadness, or anger. Then after some minutes I had lost myself in the rush of sadness and anger that had been below the surface. The end of my session the book was no recognizable and I had felt the exhaustion of running a marathon, along with the relief of feeling freed.

On the last day of our 5-day Death, Dying and Transition Workshop, Dr Kubler-Ross asked me to walk with her outside and we walked towards the ocean. She told me how proud she was of me for having the courage to allow myself to feel, experience and know that I was strong enough to come out of it with a deeper sense of live. During that walk I asked someone to take a picture of us both together. Dr Kubler-Ross continued compassion for me, allowed me to trust myself and trust her to go beyond the wall of non-engagement in the intense seminar.

Ariel Rosita King and Dr Elisabeth Kubler-Ross talking at 5-Day Residential Workshop on Oahu, Hawaii

I was proud of myself and felt the support of Dr. Kubler-Ross. She had compassion for me and my life, as well as others. We were all equally important. The workshop had such a positive impact on my views and actions in my life, and especially my work as the volunteer coordinator for the Life Foundation, that I sent Dr Kubler-Ross a letter. For the second time in my life, I wanted to give of myself to say thank you, as she has given so much to me. I sent her a letter, a copy of the song that I dedicated to her, called, "How Does It Feel?" along with proof of the copyright. During that time, I was in Europe for the summer for several months before going back to Hawaii.

To my surprise I received a letter from Dr. Kubler-Ross that thank me for the music and told me about her farm in Virginia.

Dr Kubler-Ross showed me real and true compassion, that does not need to be beautiful but real. She had compassion for all and showed me how to have compassion for myself, so that I can give it to others.

Ariel Rosita King and Dr Elisabeth Kubler-Ross at Residential Workshop on Oahu, Hawaii

The Elisabeth Kubler-Ross Center

A non-profit, non-sectarian organization
dedicated to the enhancement of life and growth
through the practice of Unconditional Love.

May 28, 1986

Rosita King
2585 Dole St.
Honolulu, HI 96822

My Dear Rosita,

Thank you so much for the lovely tape
and for the lyrics and copyright certificate.
I very much appreciate that you dedicate
this song to me and I will keep in touch
with you, after your return from Europe
and I return from Europe, which will be
sometime in October.

We are busy now with the Farm, getting the
hay in and our vegetables are growing bigger
then Findhorn's.

My love and blessings to you,

Elisabeth

Elisabeth

SOUTH ROUTE 616 • HEAD WATERS, VIRGINIA 24442 • (703) 396-3441

HOW DOES IT FEEL?

Words, music and recording by Ariel Rosita King

Sadness is a breed apart.

Show me the colour of your heart.

Red lace roses in candy fields,

How does it feel,

now that you know, it's not real?

My Darling. Oh yes life goes on.

How can I show you that your strong?

There is so much love, here to give.

Come on now, let's start to live.

Cry it out. The pain is real.

Show us both how you feel?

There is strength in honesty.

You don't have to hide when you're with me.

.

My Darling. Oh yes life goes on.

How can I show you that your strong?

There is so much love, here to give.

Come on now, let's start to live.

Sadness is a breed apart. Show me the

Colour of your heart.

16

Humanity is Courage

Dr. Matthew Raphael McVarish - Scotland

I can't help but be deeply moved by the journey we shared. Meeting and working with Dr Matthew McVarish was like encountering a bright force of nature, a man propelled by an unyielding determination to confront the darkest corners of human experience.

I vividly recall the conversations we had, where he laid bare the harrowing tale of his childhood, marred by unspeakable sexual abuse at the hands of his own uncle. The sheer magnitude of Matthew's resilience struck me to the core. Despite enduring unimaginable trauma, he refused to succumb to despair. Instead, he sought out professional help, delving into counseling and therapy to navigate the labyrinth of his own suffering.

But Matthew's journey didn't stop there. He transformed his pain into art, crafting a poignant play titled "To Kill a Kelpie," a raw exploration of the night he and his brothers uncovered the horrifying truth of their unknown shared sexual abuse. It was a cathartic act of defiance, a testament to his refusal to be silenced by shame that did not belong to him.

What truly astonished me was Dr. Matthew's decision to abandon his thriving career on a popular British children's television show to embark on "The Road to Change", a crusade to 28 countries in the European Union to raise awareness about childhood sexual abuse, and advocate for legislative reform and harmonisation.

Here was a man who could have basked in the comfort of his success, yet he chose instead to confront the darkness head-on, to ensure that no child would suffer in silence as he had.

Through Ariel Foundation International and personally we supported Dr Matthew McVarish by connecting him to and setting up participation in the diplomatic community, embassies, the United Nations, and the European Union. Yet, this was not enough because a two-year walk needs funding!

We also financially supported him, and the Road to Change, made Media contacts, and literally from Holland to Germany I drove the caravan, cooked for him, cleaned, and organised media interviews, supporting his walk in every way I could. My actions allowed me to know that I was totally committed to Dr McVarish, as he was totally committed to the cause to spread awareness about child sexual abuse and the need for harmonisation of laws of protection and accountability.

I joined Dr McVarish on this odyssey, a caravan of solidarity traversing the European Union, from Belgium to Germany, amplifying his message through interviews and community outreach. Together, we braved the challenges of life on the road, sharing meals in cramped campers and confronting our own fears in the dead of night.

I was with him day and night, and I must tell you, it was not easy. The walk was not easy for him, it was not easy for me or the people driving the van, preparing meals and caring for Mcvarish while he concentrated on walking from one city to another and one country to another. it was a labour of love. Just imagine every day getting up and doing it, whether you want to do it or not.

One memory stands out vividly: a moment of paralyzing fear as we parked by the roadside, haunted by the specter of unknown dangers lurking in the darkness. Yet, even in the grip of fear, Matthew's unwavering resolve shone through, a beacon of courage illuminating our shared path.

As we journeyed together, I found myself grappling with profound questions of humanity and resilience. What does it mean to be truly seen and acknowledged? How do we navigate the tangled web of trauma and emerge whole on the other side?

In our conversations, Matthew and I delved deep into the heart of these questions, unraveling the complexities of human experience with an unflinching honesty. We spoke of the importance of embracing our own authenticity, of finding solace in the quiet depths of our own souls.

He was able to complete the walk through 28 European Union, 28 countries. As we parted ways, I carried with me a newfound sense of purpose, inspired by Matthew's indomitable spirit and unwavering commitment to justice. His journey had become my own, a testament to the enduring power of resilience in the face of unimaginable adversity.

In Matthew's story, I found echoes of my own struggles and triumphs, a reminder that even in our darkest moments, there is always a glimmer of hope waiting to be discovered. And as I continue my own journey, I carry with me the lessons learned from our shared odyssey, a testament to the transformative power of human connection and the enduring resilience of the human spirit.

Humanity is Courage 143

Road to Change, Sponsor and Active Supporter, Ariel Foundation International

Dr Matthew McVarish, and Dr Ariel King and bagpiper
at the Road to Change sendoff in London.

*On the border between Holland and Germany,
Dr King part of the 2-person team as Driver-Cook, Media*

Dr Matthew McVarish, and Dr Ariel King on the Road in Germany

Dr Ariel King, Dr Matthew McVarish and unknown at the Scottish Castle at End of Walk

17

Humanity is Consideration

President Nelson Mandela, South Africa

While in South Africa as a Rotary Scholar, from the London School of Hygiene & Tropical Medicine, for my PhD infield research. The University of Cape Town guided my infield research on "The Policy of Getting Basic Medicines to the People in the New South Africa". As a young person I had a group of friends who were actively building the new South Africa. One of my friends was a lawyer who actively helped to re-write the constitution of South Africa. Literally a new Constitution for all people in South Africa. My friend confided in me about his work, the difficulty, and his sense of personal responsibility to get it right. I understood that we were living in an extremely important time in world history. I understood that what he was doing was extremely important and told him so.

I told my lawyer friend that I would really like to go with him one day to the Parliaments. He said that he wanted to introduce me to President Nelson Mandela. He said "I'm going to be at parliament in Cape Town. So come and I will set up a meeting for you with President Mandela." Absolutely! I was so happy!

Weeks later, we flew from Johannesburg to Cape Town to attend the appointment with President Nelson Mandela. He is such an inspiration and important person in my life. For years South Africa and its people became personal; as a teen with South Africa friends-mentors, as a university student, supporting divestiture and an end to apartheid and then as a PhD student evaluation of the policy implementation for all people had access to basic medicines.

Ariel Rosita King, and other students celebrate at the University of Hawaii Divestment in South Africa

We arrived at the capital in Cape Town and found our way to the Presidential office. My friend had to go to the Parliament for business. As I waited for my appointment time, I was also told that President Mandela was urgently called to Parliament. He would be back for our appointment. As I waited, I was then brought to another office. Behind a large desk was a man of Indian descent who smiled at me and welcomed me to the Presidents office. He sat me down and had someone bring us tea. Before I knew he was the famous "brother" of President Nelson Mandela in the Anti-Apartheid movement, he asked me about myself and my adaption to South Africa and my PhD studies. I told him about my connections to South Africa for most of my life, including the Taitz family as a child, my actively campaigning for divestment while at the University of Hawaii while an undergraduate student, and now my desire to be a part of the solution for justice in health access for the new South Africa through my PhD research.

University of Hawaii Regents OK Stock Divestment 1986

Mr. Ahmed Mohamed "Kathy" Kahtrada, introduced himself to me only as "Kit." He was part of the main five African National Congress (ANC) Anti-Apartheid team to be convicted and went to prison together with Nelson Mandela on Robbin Island. Ahmed Kathrada, an Anti-apartheid activist said he considered himself a brother to Nelson Mandela and the adopted son of Bantu Stephen Biko (Steve Biko). While waiting for President Nelson Mandela to get back from the Parliament I had the privilege of being hosted by his brother, Mr. Ahmed Kahtrada a leader in the African National Congress (ANC) and Anti-apartheid movement. During South Africa's first democratic elections in 1994, He was elected to the Parliament and served as a Parliamentary Counsellor in the Office of the President.

Since President Mandela was occupied at the Parliament with no idea when he would be free again, he showed such incredible consideration to ask the person who was a close "brother" to him to take his place. I understood that I was important too!

We sat down together to talk about the challenges of the new South Africa, President Mandela, their relationship over a lifetime and the desires for a change that was a long time coming. We talked together about how South Africa was going forward and even more importantly, how the new Government under President Nelson Mandela were focused on giving basics amenities for all people, including getting basic medicines to the people at every level of health care.

I explained to him that I was doing my PhD field research for the London School of Hygiene and Tropical Medicine (LSH&TM), as a Rotary Ambassadorial Scholar as an exchange student at University of Cape Town (UCT). My research looked at getting basic medicines to the people. After about 2 hours of sitting and talking with Mr. Kahtrada, we received a message that President Mandela was still in emergency constitutional meetings at the Parliament and would not be able to meet with me on that day. A new appointment would be set for us to meet.

Instead of disappointment, I felt a sense of wonder and privilege being in President Mandela's office and speaking to Mr. Kahtrada, who lived through the actions of the ANC, prison and even freedom and finally making south Africa a home for all. I remember reading, "Cry the Beloved Country" by Alan Paton in secondary school and being fascinated with life in South Africa and Southern African Countries.

In addition, as a teenager I became the teenage babysitter for a young South African Jewish family, the Taitz while living in a luxury building in New York. We have stayed family friends for over 45 years and still to this day. The Taitz told me about South Africa with stories and photos, that gave me a different view to the other South Africa, the beauty, the people, and the majesty of it. I learned to love South Africa before I knew how to find it on a map. Now, I have had the ultimate gift of being invited to meet the new President of South Africa and met his "brother" who "looked after me", spoke with me with honesty and hope about the future of South Africa, while waiting to meet with President Mandela.

President Nelson Mandela couldn't meet me because he was doing what he was elected to do; be a responsive President of a country that was in transition. To do everything that he could to pull the country together. The fact that I was in his appointment book, and President Nelson Mandela added me to his long list of important actions, gave me a sense of worthiness. Additionally, when he could not meet with me, he instead had me meet with his friend, brother, and colleague for over 45 year, Mr. Ahmed Kahtrada.

After a full day in Cape Town, I flew back to Johannesburg and went back home to Pretoria with a renewed hope not only for South Africa, but for humanity. Our resilience and our capacity to forgive and go forward.

When I think back on the invitation by President Mandela and my meeting with Mr. Ahmed Kahtrada, I'm so emotional about it because even though President Mandela was actively working to save a country with millions of people, after apartheid. As he was doing that, he was able to see one person and give consideration to one person. And that one person was me.

About a week later, my young lawyer friend brought me a package from President Mandela. It was a signed photo. President Mandela went further to show me my importance by sending me a signed original photo "To Rosita Warm Wishes, Mandela 1989".

In the end, my encounter with Mandela may not have unfolded as I had envisioned, yet it left me with a profound sense of gratitude and admiration. President Mandela's consideration of me and giving me the absolute understanding of my value was the ultimate unveiling of humanity.

It was a reminder that true leadership is not just about grand gestures and lofty speeches, but about the small acts of consideration that touch our lives in meaningful, often unexpected ways. President Nelson Mandela showed me that humanity is consideration for others.

Signed photo Ms. Rosita King, Best Wishes. from President Nelson Mandela 8 March 1999

Official State Photo, "Mandela" given to Dr. King at visit to Presidential Office, Cape Town

18

Humanity is Legacy

Dr. Margo G. King

Dr. Margo Geraldine King

As I stood behind the bed of my unconscious mother in the Intensive Care Unit, after neurosurgery, I understood that life is fleeting. As the only child, who father passed many years before, it was my duty to do all needed. Dr Margo G. King had an office with employees, and patients who were left to wonder what was next. Since living in Europe for almost 25 years at the time, I was challenged to understand the workings of the United States Government, legal responsibilities of my mother's doctor office, and all that needed to be done with her real-estate development projects.

For many years Dr. Margo G. King, forged her own path. As a teen mother after completing high school, she was encouraged to attend college by her Aunt Rosalie, who I was named, Rosita (little Rose) who was a nurse aid and brought me home from the hospital. Our extended family gave me care, love and spoiling while my mother attended college and worked.

Over the years she was able to work for Associate, Bachelor, Masters, and Doctorate degrees in clinical psychology. During these years she dedicated herself to children and youth specialty in her work and volunteer work with entire communities. My mother won many awards and recognitions, among many others, the Nelson Mandela Award for Community Service. As a trailblazer she held the first African American Male Experience in America Conference in New York City. The most important intellectual, sports and government men where speakers at the Conference was held at the World Trade Centre. For three years after the first conference, she held a second conference and two innovation summits for hundreds of youths in New York City.

My mother in her personal and professional life believed that healing was best with concentration on the equal pyramid of psychological, physical, and spiritual health.

Remembering all that my mother has done for others over the years. I came back to the reality of the time, and once again started to put my mother affairs in order, being told that she had very little chance of survival. I met with various people who worked with or knew my mother in one way or another. I learned who my mother was for and to so many other people. One woman told me that her teenage son died, and she went into a deep depression. My mother insisted that she go to her office for therapy free of charge. Another person, a doctor colleague told me that she gave him all the Diagnostic books and tools and taught him how to use them which allowed him to provide better and more profitable services.

Dr Ariel Rosita King and Dr Margo Geraldine King in USA

Dr. Margo King positively affected the daily lives of so many people. I was proud to know that her contributions positively affected those she gave of herself so generously. I learned about how she encouraged other to dream big and follow through with the acquisition of skills and work needed to make it happen. As I followed the path of my mother contacts to organise what was needed, I realised that the woman I know only as my mother, was more complex in her associations, her humbleness, her love of people, her service to others, her joy of life and her spirituality.

After three weeks in Intensive care, I was told that she was too sick to be sent to rehabilitation and could only me sent to a nursing home or I could take her home with me. At 3am, the hospital intensive care unit released my mother to my care. Dr. Margo King, who was the one used to giving, was now totally dependent as she would not even sit up, speak, or control most of her muscles. The neurosurgery and brain infection affected all. My mother in the back of a car with a blow-up bed and me in back with her while I friend drove us to my home in the East Coast, I understood that it was still possible for my mother to die before reaching our destination.

Dr Ariel King and Dr. Margo King at Ariel Foundation International event honouring African Ambassadors in on the US Presidential Yacht, SS Sequoia

Less than several days after reaching home, still bed-ridden, my mother still held on to her precarious life. I asked my grand-mother, Gloria Jefferson King to come see her because several time we were sure she was losing life. One evening, my mother died, said she spoke to G-d, who told her that her time was not over, and she needed to go back to finish her earthly assignment. She asked if she could stay, and G-d insisted that she go back.

The best gift I have ever received is my mother coming back from near death. Only weeks after not being able to sit up, I found my mother walking in the hall near her bedroom. I was overwhelmed with being grateful for this miracle. I said, "mom you are a miracle!" Now we were able to actively help her recovery with diet, physical therapy, message, speech therapy and family love! The months of recovery from not be able to sit up to dancing and going back to her own home after our collective Mother's Day, in which we had 4 generations in the house, taught me about determination, love, loyalty, hope, courage, family and legacy.

Dr Margo King became stronger and determined to live life again with more gusto for love, spiritualty, tenacity, courage, and a will to find a way to leave a legacy of service, education, faith, spirituality, and a belief that contributing to humanity is the greatest act of love one can give. My mother had a special talent of talking with people and very quickly understanding their pain or stuck points and devising a plan to help them have a better life for themselves.

Dr Margo G. King with her grand-daughters, Ariana-Leilani, and Victoria Anya

For twelve years after this challenging life event, I had the privilege of spending time with my mother. We spent time traveling in Europe, Africa, and at our family home in the USA that she designed. We spent time having mother-daughter talks, about being a mom, guarding and nurturing my mental health, being grateful and spiritual, and giving encouragement in my professional endeavours, especially the foundation since 2002. Most importantly being present, kind, and caring mother to my daughters, Ariana-Leilani, and Vicky Anya. My mother loved being a grandmother.

Dr Margo King passed on to me the strength to be independent in my thinking, the ability to stand alone when needed, yet the desire to stand with others in solidarity in our desire to live the best life possible.

The legacy Dr. Margo King passed on is a belief in ourselves, and others with a firm understanding that our collective humanity is the basis of a life well lived. If she had the opportunity to read this book, she would tell me how proud she is of my sharing my experiences, and to shine a light into the most important part of lives – our shared humanity as a human race.

My mother, Dr Margo King would remind me that humanity is within us all, and we need to use it, protect it, and respect it.

Humanity is the basis of who we are!

Dr Margo King and Dr Ariel King at the Senior Center for an Ariel Foundation International Senior Summit

19

Humanity is Life

Conclusion

We all want more personal development. We all want more of whatever we feel or believe we are missing in our lives. Yet, we don't realise that we already have it within us! The "more" that we want is available. It is something you already have within you!

What you are missing cannot come from outside of you but is a life source within you that is ready whenever you are to be harnessed through humanity.

We only need to be gently reminded about who we are as human beings, as in today's fast paced, online, technology centered world, we forget that at our core we are humanity in action.

Many people think that humanity encounters rarely happens. They say, "yes, but this doesn't happen to me." How do you know? You are not there to receive it? So how could you ever know if humanity encounters don't happen to you? You must be open to give yourself enough grace and time to experience your and others humanity.

We as human beings must give ourselves enough grace, care love to experience humanity encounters inside and outside of us. I had decided long ago that I was going to stop trying to be perfect, instead I was going to be fully humane! It freed me to experience all of humanity as a full person. It was a conscious decision.

I also saw so many people around me trying to be who they weren't, including myself. I found myself failing at trying to be something that I couldn't be. I like myself, and I liked people, and I wanted to be the best person I could be. Yet, there were times that I just couldn't. There are times I said, "no, I'm not going to be fair. I don't like you. That's the end of that. Sorry." I was very difficult to meet who I was, to who I was supposed to be. I felt that I was always failing or falling short. After a while I thought, "no, it's okay...Yes. Sometimes I'm not the best person. Yes. sometimes I'm the most honest person. Sometimes I'm the most selfish person. And other times I am the complete opposite. But that's okay, because I am fully human. Thus, I can at any time access and experience grace, and humanity.

Since I decided early in my life to allow myself to be fully human, the decision has been a foundation of my life. I am grateful to be fully humane because it's allowed me to not just love and accept myself, but to really be there for myself, and kind and forgiving to myself. Thus, because I am human with myself, I can see humanity and I experience humanity anywhere and at any time with anyone. In other words, humanity opens the world to me and me to the world.

I do not understand how I have met the various people highlighted and many not in this book, because it's not by design. I'm not important. I don't have any big name or talent for these prestigious people to be a part of my life and me a part of theirs. Somehow, I'm in this humanity atmosphere. Somehow, I'm there in the right place at the right time. What is interesting is that when I am with extraordinary people, it doesn't mean that I'm great or there is something special about me. What is means is that these extraordinary people know and understand that they encompass the various components of humanity aa conduit. They share their humanity rather than hoarding it for themselves. These extraordinary people, give and share Humanity because they know that in doing so, it will be multiplied and spread to others and ultimately to be passed on throughout the world.

The key is that you're not going to be able to receive it or experience humanity, without first giving it to yourself. You're not going to be in receiver mode when you haven't fully engaged who you are and your own humanity for yourself.

That's the hardest thing. Many times we are told somehow not to care for ourselves, not to do for ourselves not to think about ourselves first. And I'm not talking about like the selfish way. I'm talking about in a way to understand that we are deserving of care. We are deserving of consideration; we are deserving of love and humanity, and everything goes back to "Do you see me? Do you value me? "Do you know that my place in the world is important for the world? " When all of these questions are yes, that's all people want to be recognised in their humanity. That's literally all.

People want to be cared for with humanity. We all want to be seen, heard, recognised, and appreciated. That's what people want. It's very simple. It's not big or terribly interesting, or a huge ask or some kind of intellectual leap. It's basic and fundamental to our being human.

When we experience humanity in its purist form, it wakes us up and reminds us of our true inner being that shines and fills any, and all spaces with our positive energy.

Humanity is Confidence

Humanity is Authenticity

Humanity is Resilience

Humanity is Value

Humanity is Civility

Humanity is Respect

Humanity is Championing

Humanity is Mentoring

Humanity is Forgiveness

Humanity is Compassion

Humanity is Joy

Humanity is Connection

Humanity is Kindness

Humanity is Humility

Humanity is Responsibility

Humanity is Celebration

Humanity is Courage

Humanity is Legacy

HUMANITY IS YOU!

IF I AM NOT FOR MYSELF, WHO WILL BE FOR ME?

IF I AM ONLY FOR MYSELF, WHAT AM I?

IF NOT NOW, THEN WHEN? – HILLEL

IF NOT ME, THEN WHO? - KING

About The Author

DR. ARIEL ROSITA KING, MPH, MBA, PHD, DTM&H (UK), PHD (FRANCE), Founder and President Ariel Foundation International & Dr. King Solutions is an author, speaker, entrepreneur, Charity founder, and one of the world's most innovative humanitarians.

"Empowerment is not about giving power, but about releasing the power they already have." This quote embodies the spirit of Dr. Ariel King's work in fostering empowerment and creating opportunities for individuals and communities to thrive. Dr. King's dedication to empowering children and youth, and fostering their active involvement in international decision-making processes, has garnered widespread recognition and acclaim.

Dr. King is the Founder and President of Ariel Foundation International (www.arielfoundation.org), a non-profit organization started in 2000 with a focus on leadership, entrepreneurship, and community service. Ariel Foundation International was granted the United Nations Special Consultative ECOSOC (Economic and Social Council) Status in 2016, and NGO Observer Status at the European Parliament in 2015. The organization is registered in the USA, France, Switzerland, and Ghana.

Dr. King has made a significant impact on the lives of youth across 30+ countries on every continent. Notably, Ariel Foundation International made history by accrediting children and youth as official Delegates to the United Nations Human Rights Council in Geneva. Through her foundation, Dr. King has promoted partnerships, peace, and prosperity through entrepreneurship and education.

Dr. King is the main representative for Ariel Foundation International at the United Nations in Geneva, Vienna, New York, and Nairobi. She has also been an active member of organizations such as Women Impacting Public Policy (WIPP), the Women's Foreign Policy Group (WFPG), and various International Rotary Clubs for over 30 years.

In 2000, Dr. King established Ariel Consulting International, Inc., now known as Dr. King Solutions (www.drkingsolutions.com), a company focused on enhancing Public-Private Partnerships in international health, policy, and management.

Dr. Ariel Rosita King has over 35 years of experience in international governments, diplomacy, business, and NGOs. She has worked and lived in twelve countries and travelled to over 85 countries across Asia, Africa, the Americas, the Middle East, and Europe.

Dr. King lives by her favourite quote by Hillel, "If I am not for myself, who will be for me? If I am only for myself, what am I? If not now, then when?" This reflects her belief in acting and bearing personal responsibility. She has embraced the missing piece in this quote, realizing the importance of asking, "If not me, then who?"

www.ingramcontent.com/pod-product-compliance
Lightning Source LLC
Chambersburg PA
CBHW042030050526
44107CB00123B/1418/J